SCATTERED PINK

A DIARY OF A WOMAN IN RECOVERY

HONESTY LILLER

Liller, Honesty. *Scattered Pink: A Diary of a Woman in Recovery*

All rights reserved.

ISBN: paperback 979-8-9852741-0-3, ebook 979-8-9852741-1-0

Library of Congress Catalog Number: 2021924101

KWE Publishing www.kwepub.com

REVIEWS OF SCATTERED PINK

"In her book, Honesty shares a simultaneously heartwarming and heart wrenching story of her path to recovery. What she reveals is both refreshing and terrifying, and she has without a doubt lived up to her name. We have all been touched by addiction – and no matter how we've been touched, we can recognize our shared humanity in Honesty's words. Her lived experience proves over and over that the way out of hell is through. It is a universal testament that those who find the courage to be honest and vulnerable can absolutely rediscover themselves and come into wholeness."

—Sara Daves, Intuitive Purpose Coach

"*Scattered Pink* is a moving account of the author's life in addiction and her incredible accomplishments as a CEO and entrepreneur in recovery and will be an inspiration for women, especially women with children, in and seeking recovery everywhere. Like Liller, they can choose to grow, forgive themselves, learn, love, and "live the best damn life they can while they're on Earth."

—Alison Jones Webb, MA, MPH, PS-C, Author

"A gripping, frank, and very real tale of a woman's journey from addiction to recovery. Honesty's story is living proof that recovery restores what addiction robs-not just from the individual but from the families and community members around those in or seeking recovery. Like millions of others on this journey, Honesty's very personal story demonstrates that commitment to helping others has been an essential part of her success. A fabulous, quick read that inspires others by providing hope that recovery is not just possible but a reality in communities everywhere."

—Carol McDaid, Co-Founder, Capitol Decisions Inc. and The McShin Foundation

"A remarkable true story of triumph over life's cruelty of a person's journey through adolescence to adulthood, a simple guide to recovery from addiction, a clear understanding of hope, a must read."

—John Shinholser, Co-Founder and President of The McShin Foundation

Scattered /'skadərd/ occurring or found at intervals or various locations rather than all together.

Pink /piNGk/ Noun: the best condition or degree.

AUTHOR'S NOTE

During my active addiction, I thought I was going to die and I accepted that. It sounds morbid, but it was where I was in life. I was in love with heroin and the dysfunctional relationship I had with it. Being present in my everyday life was very difficult. Using drugs for the first time at the age of twelve, I was just trying to fit in and have fun. Then there was heroin. The crimes I would commit and the hurt I would cause the people I loved never crossed my mind in pursuit of that drug. It didn't matter. I was in love the first time it was in my body. But when I finally stayed in recovery, magic truly happened. The path and journey of my life were changed completely. I am a woman in long-term recovery from drug addiction. What that means for me is that I have been drug and alcohol-free since May 27, 2007. Learning about my soul and truly who I am has been difficult, scary, beautiful, and amazing. Being able to wake up every day and walk in my purpose is priceless. I want the same for you.

Some names and identifying details in this book have been changed to protect the privacy of individuals. However, the story, the experiences, and the words are mine alone.

To Destiny, Wyatt, and Adam
Thank you for loving me.

"Don't worry about a thing
'Cause every little thing gonna be all right.
Singing don't worry about a thing
'Cause every little thing gonna be all right."
~Bob Marley~

CONTENTS

Introduction   xiii

1. Where Do We Come From?   1
2. The Hippie Chick   7
3. My First True Love   15
4. When They Found Out   21
5. Life of Chaos   29
6. My Sweet Destiny   35
7. Heroin, Take Two   41
8. Falling in Lust   47
9. Welcome to The McShin Foundation   53
10. Human Conflicts   61
11. Mommy's Lil' Sweetie   67
12. Women Rule   75
13. A Happy Life is a Healing Life   83
14. Ew Covid   91

Acknowledgements   99
Resources   101

INTRODUCTION

If you are stuck in the past or can't forgive your parents for things that were out of your control, I get it. But, I had to have forgiveness for myself and those around me in order to heal. Sure, I could blame them for things that happened to me, but what good does it do me now? This is our one and only life on the planet. Do you want to be miserable and think constantly about what happened to you or what you have done to others? I did that for too long and now I either say "F" it or I dive in deep to forgive. Only you can decide which one will work best for you.

CHAPTER 1
WHERE DO WE COME FROM?

To be honest, I don't have many good memories as a child but the ones I do have, I hold tightly in my heart. Around age eight, my body image issues started. I was a cute and chunky child.

Feelings from my circumstances at home would pour into my soul and I would eat a bunch of junk for comfort. At the school library, I found a book about a girl like me and checked it out. I overheard my parents talking about it one night, but they never talked to me. Not really sure why I focused on my body so much as a young girl, but I did. Being raised with two sisters was fun but I never understood why they didn't have my body type.

I can remember playing with Cabbage Patch Dolls, The Smurfs, and Ninja Turtles. The innocence we had as kids was simple and easy. There were vacations to the beach. Going to Nags Head, North Carolina every summer was my absolute favorite trip. Running into the ocean was so freeing and I had no fear. We did this as a family for many years until I was about ten or eleven. Then these trips started to become not so fun. There was something *off* with my parents and I could feel it. I have always had good intuition regarding people and my surroundings.

Some of the other highlights were watching NFL football games at my Nannie's, riding bikes in the country, and going to the general store. One time as a child, I stole a piece of gum from that store and felt bad, but I never confessed. I suppose my addictive nature started earlier than I thought. Stealing was a way of life after that and I stole everything from Troll dolls to brownie mix. Being good at taking things that didn't belong to me became a talent.

We didn't have much money when I was growing up. My Deddy (most people say, "Daddy" but I call him, "Deddy") worked a few jobs while my Mama stayed at home with us. Before my Deddy left work for the day, he would call us and tell us to make popcorn for him so it was ready when he got home. We were happy to do that for him; he was a hard worker; and we loved to use the popcorn machine. My Deddy is really into music and named me after a Billy Joel song. My birth name is Honesty and for most of my life, I did not live up to it. It's kind of a depressing song, but I adore my name.

By the age of ten, I started to develop some behaviors that the normal ten-year-old doesn't have. After stealing that first piece of gum from the country store down the road from my house, my habit grew bigger and bigger. The stores really didn't have cameras back then so you could take whatever you wanted. That is exactly what I did... I had so much crap. Walking in a Rite-Aid with an empty backpack and walking out with it full was a huge adrenaline rush. One time, I got enough school supplies for the whole school year. I suppose I just wanted things other kids had, so I took them. My dresser was lined with Troll dolls, everyone of them you could imagine, I had. I was a little obsessed with those damn dolls. They were all different and that is how I felt on the inside...different. One day my Deddy came into my room and asked me, "Where in the world did you get all those dolls?" I told him that my friends gave them to me. He didn't question it and kept moving. *Maybe these things would make me popular? Like myself more?*

Make more friends? Who really knows. I just wanted and I took...wanted and I took.

People would give me lists of stuff they wanted and I would go get it from whatever store I could. It was an addiction in itself. Stealing was such a weird process. Checking around to see if anyone was looking, moving something to a different area of the store, putting it in my bag, and then looking all around again literally was a high. On one occasion, I was at Dillard's department store *(I think it was Dillard's, this was like 100 years ago)* taking some jewelry when I heard a static sound and looked to my left. It was an undercover security guard and that sound was her walkie-talkie. *Busted!!!* Those nicer stores had cameras in the mirrors that I didn't know about. This was my first time really getting in trouble and they had to call my Mama. I was eleven at this point and so scared. *Were they going to put me in handcuffs like in the movies? Was there going to be a big light in my face with a cop asking me questions?* It sucked and my heart raced. It wasn't like the movies. They just told me to give back the items, talked to me sternly, and made me go to a class on what happens when you get caught stealing. My Mama had to go with me and it was super lame. But, I didn't get charged with anything and that was pretty cool. However, that situation didn't stop me from stealing. Although, I didn't go into Dillard's for years after that. My parents didn't punish me either. My Mama kind of shrugged it off and said, "Don't do it again." Turning a blind eye to problems was common in my household.

There was obviously a void in my soul that desperately needed to be filled. Growing up, I always had some sort of emptiness in my heart. I know my parents loved me, but we never really talked about love and feelings. Fortunately, I had a few friends that were fun, cool, and helped fill that void.

From the outside, we looked like a normal family, whatever that means. But the things happening in my world at home, I kept a secret and didn't want my friends to know. My memories include a lot of yelling, screaming, slamming of doors, loud music, and not so kind words. *Maybe from the financial stress my parents were under? I don't know?* I was embarrassed, confused, and just didn't want to deal with questions from anyone. Being that young, my friends wouldn't have understood anyway. Or maybe even if they would have, their families seemed to have it all together. My friends had parents who were both usually employed. They had a routine in their homes and they all seemed to be wealthy compared to my family. One of my closest friends, Trick, was so much fun to be around and we had great times together. Her family was funny and very open with one another. I didn't know it then, but Trick would one day be a life-saving angel for me.

Looking at old photos, I always had a huge smile on my face. As a young girl, even though there were rough times, it looked as though I was happy. For some reason, my parents always dressed me and my older sister like twins. *She is three years older than me, so what the heck?*

Fortunately, we had some other traditions in our family like going to my aunt's house on Halloween to trick or treat with my sisters and cousins. On my Deddy's side, we played football together as a big family. Those gatherings always brought me joy and I really felt connected when we did things together. I loved sports, being outside, and things most boys did.

My Nannie was amazing and always made me laugh. She loved all of us. She spoke her mind without really caring what anyone thought. I admired that a lot as a kid. The memory that stands out the most is the one where I used to steal her Marlboro Reds when I started smoking. My adrenaline surged when I was sneaking in her drawer and grabbing a couple of cigs out of her pack. It was intense. Stealing from her happened after my drug addiction began. We were close until my addiction took over and then, I missed opportunities to spend time with her. Thinking of her now, it hurts my heart that I missed out on having more time with her. Frequently, cardinals come into my yard and I know that is her watching over me as well as forgiving me.

My home life continued to get worse and my parents fought which made me feel confused, scared, and traumatized. I never knew what was going to happen with them. My Mama developed her own type of illness that us girls had to live with every day. I don't have a medical term for it, but I do know it was a mental illness of some kind that made her behavior unpredictable. She lost her mom at a young age due to cancer and I think that was a part of her issues. Overall, I think my parents did the best they could with what they had but it was not a fun time when things got out of control in our home. My sisters and I would hide in the closet away from the screaming and madness. It went on for years and affected me deeply. I developed a lot of fear and got scared easily. Because of my fear, I would sleep on the floor next to where my Mama slept. I would have a pallet made for me with the box fan making a blaring sound. My fears and insecurities blossomed quickly and to this day, I still sleep with a box fan. *When I travel and forget it, there is always a trip to Walmart.*

My Deddy was gone a lot with his jobs and other activities. So, my Mama was always at home physically, but emotionally she was not there. This led to my sisters and I having a lot of freedom at a young age. My older sister's friends would hang out at our house. One time before my drug use started, one of them asked if I wanted "candy." I know now that I was being offered LSD. *He ended up being one of my many boyfriends a few years later, I can sure pick em'.* Glad I didn't take it that day though or my Ninja Turtles would have been moving all around talking to me and shit. I always wanted to be around my older sister's friends and be "cool", but she really wasn't having it. Teenagers usually don't want their little sisters pestering them when their friends are over. Who knew a year or so later, I would be "friends" with a lot of those same people that were older than me. Once I started using drugs, I had all kinds of so-called friends. Throughout my childhood, there was some serious emotional pain and as I grew older, I thought it was permanent damage to my soul.

You can't always choose your life circumstances.
But, you can learn and grow from them.

CHAPTER 2
THE HIPPIE CHICK

One of the strange things about me is that I smoked weed for a year before I ever touched a cigarette. This is not the norm. I was asked several times if I wanted a hit of weed or a beer, but I always said no. It was the early 1990s when Nancy Reagan taught us that using drugs was bad. Everyone knew the slogans "Don't Do Drugs" and "Just Say No". The anti-drug campaign was for all of society to see what happened if you got caught with drugs...You get locked up!

Therefore, I was scared to do drugs and I didn't want to go to jail. However, at that time I felt the peer pressure and eventually caved in. I saw my friends were doing it and they didn't seem to have any consequences. So, I thought I would try a little to see what would happen to me. The first day I smoked weed, I will never forget it. I was twelve years old hanging out at a friend's house. I coughed; I laughed; I loved it! I was running around their driveway and screaming with joy.

Maybe it was really good weed or maybe I was still a child trying to break free?

And then, the hippie girl in me came out. When I started

smoking weed, I truly believed that it was from the earth and it wasn't bad for me. I loved the freedom weed gave me to laugh at everything and eat everything in sight. I became known as the chunky friend because I constantly had the munchies. Sarah, (who was the sister of one of my sister's friends), and I became best friends quickly and were with each other all of the time. She did drugs and drank beer. Addiction wasn't talked about much back then. If you did drugs, you were a bad person and deserved to be in jail. That's what society taught us and so many people went to jail for a long time because they were addicted to drugs.

It is very sad actually, but we have to move forward and keep advocating for change. While some of our criminal justice system has changed, we still have a LONG way to go.

Weed, drinking alcohol, LSD, shrooms, and then cigarettes was the order of my drug use. At first, I wanted to fit in but then it became a lifestyle for me. The "friends" I hung out with were older than me. Except for Sarah, we were in the same grade. School wasn't really my thing.

While using drugs, I was there and did my work but had very little motivation to learn. I was a good little girl on paper but that's what I needed to do to cover up my drug use. If you did good, no one gave you shit and let you be. I was a bit of a bully in school. I didn't like many people, only the ones I used drugs with and my best friend. I came across as being mean but really, I was insecure and didn't know who I was. Honestly, I didn't like myself. My interactions with people were fake and I didn't care about making any other friends. I filled my body with drugs and had low self-esteem. *Add some hormones on top and you have a very dysfunctional teenager.*

Even though I wasn't super motivated to be in school, working at the school store with Sarah and her sister was a lot of fun. We were usually high which made interacting with other students interesting. *Weed made me someone that I could get down with; someone that didn't have to live up to much; just chill and sell shit at the store.* In between certain classes, we had a break and would go take bong hits real quick then head back into school. It is absurd to think about now, but it was my life. Smoking weed in the bathroom was a regular, daily thing for me. Not sure why I never got busted, I guess I had a guardian angel. Either way, I didn't care if I got caught or not. Drug dogs would come into our school randomly and sniff for drugs. One day, I turned a corner in the hallway and saw a cop with his dog. My stomach dropped and I turned around immediately. In my overalls, I had some great weed that I had gotten from a Phish concert parking lot. The dog would have sniffed it out for sure because it was very potent. Getting arrested wasn't my concern, I just didn't want them to take that weed from me. So, I quickly hid it and walked right past that dog. As soon as the bell rang, I went back to my spot and got it. "Dank" is what we used to call it and I was obsessed. It would literally stick to your finger when you touched it. Weed was very important to me and I took good care of what I had. *Doesn't everyone do that with something they love?*

At twelve or thirteen, I started going to concerts and loved it. It made me feel older than I actually was. Sometimes, I never made it into the show. The parking lot is where I could get great weed, nitrous balloons, cool clothes, and yummy weed brownies. Getting there early and staying after the show ended was the life. My parents had no idea that I went to any of those concerts. They thought I was just staying overnight with a friend and they believed me. It was exhausting sometimes, but I would wake up and do it all over again.

Experiencing LSD and shrooms was a blast at first but hallucinating is no joke, it is trippy, literally. Every time I was on acid, I never knew what would happen. One time, I ate a blue Blow Pop and when I opened my mouth it looked like a never-ending tunnel. Taking acid was a big risk but everyone was doing it. On my thirteenth birthday, my friends were dropping me off at my house so I could do the whole family thing with cake and ice cream. As I got out of the van, one of my friends said, "Open your mouth." At that moment, some acid was popped into my mouth which made for an eventful birthday celebration. My ice cream was in a Strawberry Shortcake bowl and it looked like the ice cream was melting her face. I was seeing the visual trails of everyone as they moved and the candles were out of this world. I went to my room to lay down because I needed to get the hell out of there.

Have you ever been tripping on acid in front of your family and you were trying to hide it from them? It is not a good time at all. With acid, your body builds up a tolerance which means you have to do more and more to feel its effects. Those effects are nuts.

I was doing so much of it in a short period of time. The last time I touched acid, it made my stomach hurt as I was coming down off of it. By the time I was fifteen, I told myself I wouldn't do it anymore and I never touched it again.

In addition to going to concerts, I spent my free time at Fall's Hole which was a bunch of rocks leading down to a body of water. At that bottom, there would always be a big bonfire, alcohol, and a lot of weed. Sometimes, I didn't have a clue as to why I was there because everyone was older than me. *Is this what other thirteen-year-olds did? I don't think so.* I felt accepted and didn't cause any drama. Although, not everyone hanging out there was a good person. There was an older man who tried to have sex with me while I was completely hammered out of my mind on alcohol. One of my friends came in and saved me. Throughout my life, I have had many guardian angels in the form of humans. *Thank you, Joe!*

Going to downtown Richmond was the cool thing to do. My friends and I would ride up and down Broad Street. In random parking lots, most everyone was using some type of drug or alcohol. There were lots of fights and loud music blaring all the time. It was both explosive and insane. Back then, my mouth was bigger than my ability to back up my words with action. I probably would've gotten my ass kicked but thankfully, I had older friends to fight for me.

One summer, I practically lived at Sarah's house. I would only come home once a week or so to wash my clothes. No one in my home really noticed. I guess they just assumed I was having fun. That summer there were late nights, parties, and lots of different people coming in and out. I thought I was living the life! In the beginning of my drug use, I thought I would smoke weed forever, go to concerts, and just dance. Show after show, drug after drug, and drama after drama, that lifestyle only lasted for a few years.

My first boyfriend, Steve, was the love of my life. Well at age thirteen, I thought he was. He was the world to me and I revolved my life around him, around us. Basically, he was my "first" everything. Our relationship was young love, young brains, young souls, and young hearts. I didn't know what a healthy relationship looked like, so ours was not healthy. I treated him badly and I truly feel bad about it now. We were together for about a year. I was young and didn't know who the hell I was. I wanted someone to complete me. His family loved me and I loved them.

Using drugs and alcohol in a relationship brought fighting, making up, and fighting again. We had no clue what we were doing. Neither one of us had any healthy relationships in our life. Eventually, we parted ways but still remained friends and did a lot of drugs together.

I was taught "Crack Is Whack," but I tried it anyway at the age of fifteen. It made me feel funky and I totally felt like I needed more as soon as I finished smoking it. It created a whole world of chaos for me where I would literally be awake for an entire weekend. One time, I thought I was dying and couldn't catch my breath. I was eating Doritos and my heart started racing. The friends I was with at this time were doing it, so I thought why not? Again, I had guardian angels because obviously, I did not die.

Once crack entered my life, I started to separate from my hippie friends but I went back and forth between the weed smokers and the crack smokers. *What a life...good grief!* Now fifteen, I was able to get a job after school to support my drug use. I worked with Sarah and her sister and actually enjoyed working. My new crowd of friends did a lot of powder cocaine. *And, yep...me too.* I thought it was what I needed to do to fit in. Graduating high school was important to me but only because I wanted to get the hell out of school. So, I took English 12 in summer school when I was sixteen and graduated that summer with Sarah. My job hired me full-time and I was set. That income was crucial for my drug use. I didn't mind fending for myself, it gave me strength even though I spent most of my income on drugs. There was no opportunity for college because I was so focused on drugs. I had no desire to do anything but work and use. *Didn't everyone do that?* My job paid okay, but I needed more money for my drug-using lifestyle. The best way to do that was to sell drugs myself. I did for a bit, but my supplier eventually went away. Being a sixteen-year-old drug dealer sounds strange now, but it was my truth. My drug use was always outside of our family home. *Well, at least for the most part.* Don't get me wrong...the bathroom was my favorite place to escape and use if I was stuck at home for any reason. Nothing like blowing into a toilet paper roll with a dryer sheet to cover up the smell of weed. *At least I thought it covered it up.*

"Don't Do Drugs" and "Just Say No" aren't phrases that I say.

Have open conversations about drugs and alcohol with those you love.

CHAPTER 3
MY FIRST TRUE LOVE

My need for acceptance and wanting to fit in always took over. There I was, not loving myself. I didn't like how I looked or who I was. Lowrider trucks, bass bumping, and lots of drugs was a perfect combination to make those feelings all go away. Now, Sarah had a long-term boyfriend and she was with him all the time so I had to find new friends to be around. Easy as changing my clothes, I could change my surroundings and be someone that I was not, which led to hanging out in the Food Lion and McDonald's parking lots and bumping hip-hop music. My time was focused on bong hits and cigs. Weed was my "go to" drug and we had a very special relationship for many, many years. Somedays, I wonder how in the hell I have any brain cells left. I started using it when I was twelve, which is basically a baby brain. It didn't have the chance to develop correctly because of all the chemicals I put in my body. This brain I have now though, *WOW*, it is unbelievably intelligent. *Maybe the cells grew back? Who knows?*

Most of my friends were guys and I had very few girl-friends at this point. I thought the people I called "friends" had my back, loved me, and respected me. Well, in many cases with some of these guys that did not happen. Some were mean, some were annoying, and some were straight up losers. But I didn't care, I wanted to be liked and I needed acceptance even if it was from some dumb dumbs.

I was the queen of covering up my feelings and shrugging them off, but deep down I was screaming inside. My parents never really taught me how to handle or process feelings so I usually covered them up, did more drugs, and moved on. There were many days that seemed like a blur because I just didn't want to feel. I was still a little girl in a teenage girl's body. And that body, I didn't like or love at all. All of the girls I was around were skinny and I was always the chubby one. I didn't really care because doing drugs helped me gloss over a lot of my negative self-image. When I wasn't high, there were still mirrors and I didn't like what was looking back at me.

My first car accident happened with this crew of friends and I got all jacked up. This was the first time opiates entered my body. The doctor gave me these pills after I got stitched up. They helped with the pain and they helped me avoid life for a week. Who knew that the taste of opiates would be the beginning of what would later become the real love of my life. After the accident and all the dumb shit I went through with this crew, I slowly phased myself out of their lives. Some of them got on my damn nerves.

Throughout these last teenage years of my life, I would see old friends and reconnect. Little did I know, they were all using heroin. The thought never crossed my mind that I would use it, *NEVER*. Smoking weed was my jam and I didn't need anything else. When one of my friends overdosed and died, it hit our community hard.

We are in the middle of an opiate epidemic now, but in 1997 there were people dying from it too.

This has been a problem for a long, long time unfortunately. We all grieved together. The way I dealt with it, is the way I dealt with everything, drugs and more drugs. This void was filled easily and daily.

After the death of my friend, two of those so-called guy friends and I were on my Mama's front porch in the country. I had spiraled downward and started dabbling with crack again. I was smoking a blunt with crack in it and one of my guy friends told me to try the heroin so I wouldn't "geek" off the crack. This meant that I wouldn't crave more crack because the heroin would counteract with it. That day on my Mama's porch, I fell in love with what would be the love of my life for many years to come. They put it in a dollar bill, rolled up another bill for me, and handed it to me. I looked down and didn't even question it, I took a big sniff. The taste in the back of my throat and in my nostril wasn't that great, but I quickly learned to love it. I can taste it now as I am telling you my story. Heroin made me feel warm, numb, and carefree. I entered a whole different world. A world I didn't know existed, a world I didn't want to leave.

Not long after that someone who was very close to me and my family overdosed. His death was one of the worst things I have ever been through because we were super close. He was like my brother. And this one was different, this one was family. At his funeral, I was a mess. I was the loudest cryer in the room. This one hurt. That day I swore I would stay away from anyone using heroin and I knew in my heart I would never use that drug again.

That promise I made to myself didn't last a week. Feeling free was what I needed. Heroin made life easier. Heroin made life whole. Heroin made life worth living. It sounds insane and it was.

The next nine years of my journey were rough, sad, empty, and resilient. Being in love was something I truly did not know how to handle. When my body and soul fell in love with heroin, it was an adventure in and of itself. In the beginning I started slowly and carefully because I was continuously reminded in my mind that two of my friends had recently died from a heroin overdose. I didn't want to die but I didn't want to stop using it either. At the age of seventeen, I thought I had life all figured out. If I only did a little, I wouldn't OD (overdose). That worked for a few months.

I didn't use it every day. Instead, I smoked a ton of weed daily and I can't express enough how much I loved it. That was until...heroin kicked the shit out of that love story. I transitioned completely out of every group of friends I had and found some people older than myself to befriend in Downtown Richmond. We listened to music by the Grateful Dead and Bob Marley, smoked weed, and chilled out. An older man moved in with my new friends and I found out quickly that he sold drugs... that's right, the drug. At that point, my goal in life was to get what I wanted, so this little girl did just that. The older man and I clicked immediately with my winning personality and I became one of his customers...*well kind of.* Most of the time, he gave it to me for free and I thought he was nice or it was leftovers. In this house, I did so many dangerous things daily that it began a pattern in me that made me lose control. The neighborhood wasn't that great and this little girl should've been at home. But there, I felt like I was twenty-five. I was trying to fit in and be myself but unfortunately, using drugs and wanting to get more drugs didn't let me be who I wanted to be. I got along with everyone, but I was also fake as shit. I knew what to say and do to ultimately get to my end goal...drugs. Lying came naturally for me and lies flew out of my mouth constantly. *In addiction, there was no way to live up to my birth name, no freaking way.*

A going-away party was being planned for one of our friends that was going to jail. *Don't most people throw parties like this?* Probably not, but we were excited and there were lots of Jello shots to be made. Beforehand, my friends and I went downtown to an outside music venue.

There, I saw my old friend, Trick, from my pre-drug days. I invited her to the party later and put her phone number in my beeper clip. *Yep...beeper clip. I had a sweet teal one and loved it.* Trick and I parted ways. I was ready to party. It started with lots of Jello shots, I think some benzos, and then I called my "friend," the older man, the drug dealer. By this time, I was so messed up that I don't even remember calling him or the rest of this story.

I was told after I woke up that he came to the party, gave me heroin, and I sniffed it. Trick told me later that I called her and told her I was dying. She had the address I had given her earlier and sped over to help me. Everyone at the party was high, using something, or on probation. No one wanted to call 911 to help me for the fear of getting arrested. So, their bright idea was to drag me around the house as I was overdosing with the hope that I wouldn't die. When Trick arrived at the house, she came in and called 911 immediately. She helped to save my life. *Told you, she was my guardian angel.* An off-duty cop who lived in the neighborhood came right over when he heard the call. He gave me mouth-to-mouth resuscitation until the ambulance arrived. The emergency responders threw me on a stretcher and shot me up with Narcan, an opiate reversal drug that should save you from an overdose.

Do you believe in the afterlife? During all of this, my mind was gone but I remember seeing a light and my friend that had just passed away. Everything was beautiful but it didn't last long because I woke up and remembered that I was on earth. My body tried to jump off of the stretcher as soon as the meds hit my system. *Have you ever seen Uma Thurman in Pulp Fiction when they bring her back to life from her OD? That's exactly what it felt like.* They pushed me back down and threw blankets on me because I was freezing. With all of the chatter and loud sirens, I had no idea what was going on. My only thought was that I still had heroin in a dollar bill in the beeper clip in my pocket. No criminal charges for this chick, I dumped the rest of the heroin on the ambulance floor when no one was looking. *Have you ever felt so helpless but yet still thought you had all the answers?* This was one of those times for me.

Find the real meaning of "Friend" for yourself.
Don't underestimate your worth.

CHAPTER 4
WHEN THEY FOUND OUT

You can imagine what happens when a seventeen-year-old overdoses on heroin and goes to the hospital. That's right...they call your parents! When I was in the hospital, I couldn't stop throwing up. The entire experience was miserable. So many emotions and thoughts were running through my head. Seeing my sisters and parents in that hospital room, literally broke my heart. There were two things I knew. First, my family was now "in the know" about my drug use. Second, it would be difficult to cover up doing drugs now that they knew. My sisters took it harder than I thought they would. I wouldn't wish that on anyone. It was rough. My heart sank and if I could have thrown up again, I would have. *Is this real? Is this me? Did I do this to them? Their facial expressions will never leave my mind.* The fear I put in them was horrible and at the time, I truly felt bad. There should've been a pause button or fast-forward so I didn't have to feel anything at that moment. This was not a movie or a show on Netflix, this was my life. The positive thing that came out of this, was my first real memory of my parents telling me they loved me.

After I was discharged, my parents tried to get me help by taking me to a local doctor for detox. My Mama had to give me shots in my butt for a couple of weeks. This OD made my parents question everything I did. I was working for my friend's parents when this happened. This is the same friend that was renting the house where I overdosed. Needless to say, it was super awkward when I went back to work. *Like, super awkward.* I thought she was going to keep it from her parents, but she didn't. They knew what happened and that I was getting treatment but it was never the same.

When you overdose, the cops usually get involved. They showed up at my house and asked where I got the drugs. I didn't remember calling my drug-dealing friend, so I lied and said that I got the drugs from a neighborhood downtown. I drew a map of "God knows where" and said someone on the corner sold it to me. Getting drugs on the corner became true later in life, but for now, I didn't want to get my drug dealer arrested. *How would I get easy access to heroin if he was locked up?* Lucky for me, I didn't hear from those cops again.

Another good thing that came out of this part of my life was meeting my Deddy's girlfriend, Derby. I knew my Deddy was with someone else because he was barely ever home for years. *I had to grow up very quickly in my house and I was no dummy.* My parents should have divorced much sooner than they did but I guess they stayed together for us girls. My overdose opened the door for my Deddy to introduce us to our two twin half brothers as well. They were about seven years old and super cute. There was no judgement from me because I was so screwed up myself. People make choices that affect those around them and these boys were a gift to our family.

Derby took me to my first 12-Step meeting soon after the

OD. I was scared and hesitant but I knew it would make them happy if I tried it out. As I went into my first meeting and looked around, everyone in the room was much older than me which made me very uncomfortable. I only attended a couple more meetings, then I never went back. Even after my detox and the ordeal I had been through, I was back hanging around the same old friends. My parents asked me a lot more questions when I left the house, but more lies came out of my mouth. *I was lucky I wasn't named Pinocchio because my nose would have been miles long.*

Back downtown with my so-called friends, I did a little heroin at a time because I didn't want to OD again but again that didn't last long. My drug dealer friend was right there when I needed anything, so why not? There was partying and staying up all night and I was constantly exhausted, but I kept repeating the same behavior. Being a good friend to others was one of my better qualities in the beginning of my heroin addiction. I would share my heroin and make sure my people weren't getting dopesick if I could help it.

Soon after, I left my first job only holding random jobs here and there for a paycheck to support my habit. On the outside, I had to appear as if I was doing okay so my parents wouldn't question my daily activities. Unfortunately, all of the people I was spending my time with didn't have much direction in their lives. We got high, smoked, burned ourselves with our cigs when we nodded out, listened to music, and nodded out some more. *What a life...*

This went on for a few months until my "friend", the drug dealer, finally got what he wanted. One night, I woke up and he was on top of me taking advantage of me in a vulnerable situation. I just laid there because I didn't know what else to do. My brain started going berserk. *Was this really happen-*

ing? Did he just rape me? I knew it happened. I knew I didn't deserve it. When it was all over, I got up and went home even though I probably shouldn't have driven. I needed to get the hell out of there. I was living with my Mama and little sister but I never told them. I never told anyone until years later. My time was about up with that crew anyway and this was a good reason to part ways with those friends. I chose to revert back to my former friends that were all still using. It was safer, but still an insane life.

Finally, I was eighteen and a legal adult. I made it. This also meant if I got arrested, I would go to big-girl jail. I became as careful as I could with my crimes and my drug use. *Can I say guardian angels again? Amen!* Again, most of my friends were men and I hooked up with most of them. This behavior goes all the way back to not loving myself enough to be alone. As a woman, it was easy to seek acceptance from men. Most of the time, I wasn't emotionally present. I was just looking for someone to like me, to love me, and to care about me.

Initially, I was back in a relationship with Steve, my very first boyfriend, for a bit but this time it was different. I felt like I needed to prove something to him. When we were together before I was such a baby, only thirteen years old. Now years later, I felt as if I had lived a lifetime already. It was if we were meant to be together...*well maybe*.

I started hanging out with all these guys and then "poof", they were all gone. Approximately thirteen of my friends were part of a county-wide "sting" and they all got arrested. Basically, someone wore a wire and bought drugs from all of them. Steve ended up in juvenile detention because he was brought up on charges from when he was underage. I would write to him every week and take any phone call I could get.

He was there for a long time. Being the great girlfriend that I was, I cheated on him. I felt I had to because I needed a partner in my life to feel complete.

These guys were nothing like who I would be with today but being alone wasn't really an option for me.

Thankfully, today I know I have exactly what I need with my husband, a partner for life.

With all of my friends being in jail, I was left to hang out with random people, random drug users, and other drug-using friends. During my addiction, I never had any friends that were sober, ever. Most weeknights I was at the local jail visiting all my guy friends that were locked up. It was interesting. I could visit one a day each night of the week. *Talk about dedication.* Even though I was nodding out in the waiting room every night, I still pulled it together long enough to chat with them for thirty minutes. I wrote letters often and I would send them tons of pictures.

Loyalty was another good quality that I developed during this time with the exception of being loyal to Steve. All of these guys did about a year in jail and then we were right back at it. Steve and I broke up after I told him everything I was doing. I totally get it, but he was locked up. My justification for things I did wrong to people was an art as well.

While they were all in jail, I worked at a local restaurant which helped me meet new friends. Being with these new people was exciting and different because they did not use heroin. Even though I still did when I wasn't around them or when I went to the bathroom at work, they didn't know. I enjoyed working at the restaurant, and cash tips were the bomb! One day, my drug dealer came in to eat and left me heroin for my tip, even better! All of my drug dealers really liked me. I thought it was because I was nice. But now, I know it was because they just wanted to keep me as a customer.

There were times at work when I was so high I literally nodded out in front of the screen putting orders in. I used the same excuse of being "tired" for over a year. No one ever questioned it because I always showed up, worked hard, stayed late, and the customers loved me. Eventually, I slowed down when my withdrawals from heroin got worse. I decided to tell my friend at work about my heroin use. There was no judgment, but she did worry about me. Soon after that, the man I was dating at work found out. That didn't go well. I walked into the kitchen and overheard him making fun of me because I used heroin. Not sure if it was because he was hurt, or mad, or he was just a jerk. We stopped talking and it became weird between us. I had to work to support my habit and regrettably, he was there all the time. I ignored him and tried to do my best at the job but I had lots of excuses to tell my bosses as to why I was late, leaving early, or why I did not show up at all. Being a woman, I made up the usual lies like, " I just had a miscarriage" or "it's that time of the month." Every time I lied, it was dramatic like in a movie. It was nuts! They always believed me, but the real reason was either I was really dopesick or I needed to go meet my dealer.

Coming home to sleep and shower was the only time I was there. My Deddy was with his girlfriend. My sisters were living their own lives. My Mama was in her own world. There were family get-togethers, holidays, and all that jazz. I put on a good face, lied through my teeth, and showed up to what I could. I was just a human shell walking around in this world, not really knowing who I was or what the hell I was doing. All I knew was that I needed heroin to survive. By now, I had a couple of people who came to me to get their heroin because they were too scared to get it for themselves. When I hit nineteen years old, there was a younger man that came to me for some. *This turned out great, you think?*

Sometimes people hurt you or take advantage of you. You have to keep going to survive.

CHAPTER 5
LIFE OF CHAOS

Having a man in my life was convenient and Stewart was just that, convenient. Our relationship was founded on drugs. He came from a broken home with childhood problems of his own, so we connected on many levels. From the very beginning of our relationship, we jumped in head first using drugs every day and we were completely inseparable. This was not like other flings I had in the past. I thought I was in love but did I really know what love was? None of my numerous relationships before had lasted. The relationships I saw growing up made me believe that it was very hard to be in one which is probably why I didn't stay in any one of them too long. I would get bored or want something fresh and new. And let's get real, it was all about whoever had the best drugs. Throughout the whole six years we were together, we were very "lovey-dovey"…at least when we were high. This was a very dark time in my life because of constantly using whatever opiates or weed we could get our hands on. Even though heroin was always my number one choice. It was very rare but sometimes we did normal couple things like go to dinner or a movie.

He had dropped out of high school and took odd jobs. I was still somewhat employable and continued working at the restaurant. If I was going through withdrawal, he would bring me dope so I could keep it moving on the job. Everyone at my work seemed to like him and he definitely filled a void in my life. Also, we would work for his stepdad repairing things at people's homes.

That was a freaking mess because we were always high or in withdrawal. We always managed to screw something up which pissed his stepdad off. If I had a day off or we weren't working for his stepdad, we had to find a way to get money. This was my introduction to pawn shops. I had seen them in movies and never thought that I would get desperate enough to have to sell items of mine or someone else's that I stole. But there we were, getting pennies for something worth much more. We needed to get whatever we could in order to go straight to the drug dealer.

We tried multiple times to stop using drugs during the first couple of years of our relationship. I got baptized hoping the water would wash away my desire for drugs, but it didn't. Shit, we even drove to Florida all night to try to detox on our own at his dad's house. Unfortunately, that didn't go over too well. We stayed one night, stole his father's weed, and headed back to Virginia. The whole car ride back was miserable because we were both in withdrawal. We had no money and had to steal gas to get all the way home. It was a nightmare. At one point, we ran out of gas on the highway exit ramp. He was being stubborn and wouldn't walk to try to get help. It was pitch black and cold but I walked by myself with a blanket around me down the exit ramp to the interstate. It sucked! I was scared for my life. I waved down a tractor-trailer truck driver and he pulled over. As he got out of the truck, I saw him zip up his pants. I thought, *Oh Shit...I am about to get murdered.* Luckily, just the opposite happened. He called the State Police and they helped us with getting gas. As soon as the cop was gone, we went to the gas station across the street and stole more. *Insane!* We found our way back to Richmond and gave my car to our drug dealer for a few days. We had to do something to get our drugs and giving my car away was our only hope.

There were many things I didn't want to do but had to do throughout my life. However, this miserable life...consumed my existence. We were criminals and not very good human beings. During this whirlwind, I got pregnant. At first, I didn't really know that I was pregnant because when you do drugs your whole cycle gets jacked up. Your body doesn't know how to function correctly at all. But I knew something wasn't right. I went to the doctor and they gave me a test. It was positive. *Talk about being freaked out!* I was only nine-teen or twenty, I can't remember. Weeks later when they did an ultrasound, there was no heartbeat. At first, I was sad, but then I was relieved. There was no way I could be a mom, not now, not ever. God knew I wasn't ready I suppose, so I had a miscarriage. All I cared about was getting the pain meds after the procedure. I never grieved. We moved on quickly as if it was just a bump in the road of our crappy life.

When I think about this day now I get sad, but I truly know that a child wouldn't have had a great upbringing with parents like us at the time.

Shortly after that, I lost my job at the restaurant. There are only so many lies you can tell at one job and I told them all. *This began my life of panhandling.* Being a woman, I could get so much more money than Stewart. Some days, I would end up with hundreds of dollars. I know...not a great way to make a living. I did not care and I was great at pulling people's heartstrings.

Being totally addicted to heroin meant that I had to have it every day, all throughout the day. That meant I needed money. Keeping a real job was hard and my addiction interfered with my work schedule. Stewart and I figured out so many, different ways to get money. They were not fun; they were not nice; and they are things I never want to do again. As I remember the past, it truly feels like another life, like I am watching a movie. A movie filled with the hurtful things I did not only do to my own body, but to people and places. Heroin wouldn't let me stop and it breaks my heart to think about it.

I put on a good show when I was around my family and they quickly accepted *(more like tolerated)* Stewart because they knew I wasn't going to leave him. There was a lot of daily drama and pain. It was the typical life of someone who didn't care about themselves or what other people thought.

It's incredible to me now that this was twenty years ago. So many feelings still come up to the surface when I think back on those days.

Not having a job but having a social security number, I ruined my credit by maxing out any credit card that approved me. I may not have had cash, but I had credit...*SOLD!* Back then you could get five separate cell phones and lines in your name. I not only gave those phones I bought on credit out to my drug dealers but also took all of them clothes shopping.

If you know someone that is using drugs, take their credit cards ASAP. They will thank you later, hopefully. The insanity of addiction is the constant pain you feel but you keep doing it anyway hoping something will be different. If you don't love who you are, it is a difficult cycle to break.

I was still reverting back to that little girl that didn't like the way she looked, her weight, her hair, her face. Having a healthy relationship with someone was something I just did not know how to do. So, I stayed with him and lived a life of disgust.

The first time I put a needle filled with heroin in my arm was scary, but I did it anyway. Once that blood came into the needle, I pushed and the drugs were soaring through my veins. I was in heaven. I loved it but I was scared to die at this point in my addiction, so I didn't shoot it daily. But, I sure did sniff a lot of it!

Stewart had robbed a drug dealer, crossed a line, and we got caught. They tried to pull him out of the car to beat him up, but I gave them my last $20 to save him. It was a complete nightmare and it scared the shit out of me. Did it stop me from going to the same area to find heroin? *NO.* For me, it was just another day of chaos. My morals were very low and I did things that I would never do today. It took a long time for me to work through that pain.

At our family Christmas party, I would army crawl through the room where the purses were kept to see if anyone had cash in their wallets. I was like Rambo with sweat and grit getting rug burn. *CRAZY!* Somehow, my parents found out I was using drugs again. To appease them, I entered a methadone clinic. Stewart and I went every day to get our daily dose, did our acupuncture, a group therapy session, and then went to McDonald's for a caramel sundae. *Damn, I loved those caramel sundaes.* Some said methadone was just trading one drug for another. All I knew was that I wanted something in my body that would make me not feel, not have to be myself, and not go through withdrawal. However, we didn't stop other drugs like weed, benzos, and alcohol.

Mixing them all together was a big "no-no", but by now I didn't give a crap. We made new friends at the clinic and we were living with his parents. Life was getting a little better without using heroin. The worst part of going to this clinic was the therapy. *Oh my gosh*...I dreaded that and I cried every session. I hated talking about my feelings and the shit that I did because of my drug use. Having family sessions with my Deddy and Derby made me want to puke. I knew I caused them a ton of pain, but I didn't want to talk about it. I wasn't ready to dive in and have the hard conversations. This clinic life was short-lived when I found out I was pregnant again. I was in shock since I already had a miscarriage while using drugs the year prior. Everyone involved wanted me to stay on methadone my whole pregnancy because it would be better for the baby instead of detoxing. I thought I had all the answers like I was a medical professional. I said, "Absolutely not!" I was not putting drugs in my baby. I left that clinic and never went back.

Heroin was up my nose within a week.

I know, I know, mother of the year, where's my trophy?

Pain is in our lives for a reason, sometimes you just have to push through the pain.

CHAPTER 6
MY SWEET DESTINY

I thought being pregnant was a sign that I would change my behavior. I thought that I would love my baby more than I loved anything. *I thought wrong.* Growing up, I was told that God gives you babies as gifts and that they are miracles. But, my need for heroin was stronger than my need to be a mom.

This chapter was the most painful to write. But today, I am a very proud, decent mom because I was able to forgive myself.

When you have a human being growing inside your body, you are supposed to eat healthy, exercise, rest, and do all of the things those parenting books tell you to do. I read none of them. I kept using and pretending that being pregnant wasn't happening. The morning sickness never came, but the dope sickness did. Being dopesick is like you have the flu times 100 which includes sweating, puking, restless legs, and lots of other bodily functions that suck. I can't even count how many times I have been dopesick nor do I want to ever feel that way again, it is pure hell.

When you use drugs while pregnant it is a constant emotional battle. I asked myself many questions. *Why can't*

I stop? Am I hurting this baby? Do I care? Yes, I care, but do I really? I was in denial trying to justify my actions. I thought I would always be a drug user and would never stop. As a pregnant woman, I got more money panhandling. I was able to lie with a straight face, and everyone believed me. As I started showing, I had no clue how in the world Stewart and I were going to support this little human. We were barely working and had very little money, if any. Panhandling got me the money I needed daily for drugs, so I stuck with that for as long as I could. There were times that I would look down at my belly and just think. *WTF is going on, is this really happening?* My days ran into each other and life went by without me really being present in it. My belly got bigger and bigger. It was too late to turn back. Sometimes, I got excited about the thought of being a family and how we would change once the baby was born. That was truly a false hope. Most twenty-one-year-olds I knew were partying or starting a career. Here I was pregnant and addicted to heroin. I felt like the child growing inside me didn't have a chance. *Ugh, this is so hard to type...*

On the outside, I wanted everything to be normal so I kept all of my doctor's appointments. I would show up and answer all of their questions with a smile then rush out of there to go use again. During each visit, I would pee in a cup and I swore they were drug testing me. Instead, they were just checking my blood sugar levels. My addiction made me paranoid. I literally thought they were testing me for drugs and continuing my appointments knowing full well I was using. My mind went bananas as if this was a pass for me, a way out, and they were okay with it all. That is how I thought. *Insane!* My addiction got worse because of the shame I felt. I assumed I would die or someone would take my baby from me, so I kept using and using. There was no turning back or starting over, I was all in.

Baby showers and family events were very unpleasant but I had to keep up the charade. While pregnant, the feeling of desperation engulfed me. I had so much heartache that I cried all the time. I needed to do more to numb my pain. Dangerous situations seemed to follow me everywhere I went. Stewart and I ripped people off continuously. One day while trying to find drugs, we were spotted by a drug dealer that we robbed. We took off in my Mama's car and I floored it. We were now officially in the *Fast & Furious*. We flew in the air going over potholes and hit our heads on the roof of the car flying through the streets. I was the one driving and my poor pregnant belly went all over the place. It was frightening, but we got away.

And my sweet Mama, I manipulated the hell out of that woman. She was so excited for her first grandchild and I took advantage of that constantly. Your morals and values go out the window when you are addicted. I would steal her money right in front of her and then help her look for it. She must have thought she was losing her mind. I always had a story to tell in order to shift the finger from being pointed at me so she would believe me. Once while eating lunch at a restaurant, my Mama got up to go to the restroom and I snatched all the cash from the table for the bill. The waitress chased us out to the parking lot. When we went back in, I blamed a "shady looking" waiter and we left after some embarrassment. But, I didn't give up the money and I got what I needed. The progression of my addiction was baffling. I was able to sit there and lie with a straight face in front of anyone. It was easy but this was not normal. This was drug addiction.

From time to time, we had to take a cab to get our drugs. At nine months pregnant, I would run after I got out of the cab because we could not pay the cab driver. Then if needed, I would jump out of the house window once home to get away from the cab driver if he came to our front door. We didn't own a car and we didn't have a penny to buy one.

A few days before my daughter was born, Stewart's mom went out of town to take care of a family member. While she was there, she passed away. That threw the whole family into a whirlwind of pain, sadness, fear, and anxiety. *And what did we do to cope? More drugs.* The night I went into labor was the night of his mom's funeral and I took some drugs to calm me down. When my stomach started hurting, I thought it was the drugs. Fortunately, his brother took us to the hospital. It was time, I was going to be a mother. On the way to the hospital, I was high and scared. I don't remember much but wanting to puke. *In the movies when a woman's water breaks, the husband grabs the overnight bag and tries to make the woman feel better by doing all that breathing crap.* Well, that was not my story.

We made it to the hospital safely and then, everything went wild. To this day, I don't know exactly what happened but whatever they gave me, made me go into withdrawal a 1,000 times over. I jumped over the hospital bed trying to strangle Stewart. *I wanted to kill him.* The nurses came in and tried to calm me down but it just wasn't happening. I was pissed off, in major withdrawal, and in labor all at the same time. It would have taken an exorcism to fix this situation. There was no priest so I had to tell them that I was using heroin for most of my pregnancy and I needed their help. The nurse gave me methadone throughout the night. I was in and out of consciousness until the next morning. My Mama came into the room and I felt so horrible I didn't even care that she was there. I was giving up and I was screaming like a lunatic because I was having a baby that I was unprepared to raise. It was scary shit. My Deddy told me later about how I was mean to the nurses. After a night of hell, my stomach started to hurt and my contractions began. Even though I was drugged up, I still felt them and I knew I would never want to do this again. The doctor and nurses rushed in within seconds. I pushed twice and out came this beautiful baby girl. My daughter was born, 7lbs 4oz even though I did not gain much weight during my pregnancy. I believe she had a guardian angel to be born at an ideal weight.

There was my "Destiny".

Her father walked into the room right after she was born. He missed everything. But there I was, a mom. So many questions raced through my head. *What was a mom anyway? Was I supposed to take care of this girl for the rest of my life? How was I going to do it? Was he going to help? Was I going to stop using heroin? Was I going to die and leave her one day? Could I do this?*

They took her to the NICU immediately because she was born in withdrawal. My daughter and I were both withdrawing. I did this to her...*me*. I felt like the biggest piece of shit in the world. She had to stay in the hospital for two weeks and I was there every day with her. Before I got discharged, social services obviously paid me a visit. You can't just have a baby born in withdrawal and get away with it. There were questions I had to answer and they did one home visit when I left the hospital. They said I could keep her if I went directly to a methadone clinic. *Methadone again! Damn it!* Of course, I agreed because I didn't want them to take her. Even though I had no clue how to take care of her myself.

When I was leaving the hospital, there was tension in the air with my parents. My Mama still believed all my lies even though she knew Destiny had drugs in her system. My Deddy and Derby were in the hallway too and all hell broke loose.

They were pissed, scared, and more pissed. There was a lot of screaming and name-calling. *Did I say they were pissed?* I know I was a huge disappointment and I know they hated Stewart. There was nothing they could do though, the state was letting me keep her. *Well, they gave me a chance to keep her.* It was up to me to make some changes now. It was clear that the nurses thought I was a horrible mother and I felt that way too. I cried constantly as I held her in my arms. Looking down at her sweet innocent face made me so happy and also so sick. Knowing I did this to my child was the worst feeling in the whole world, the worst. She was so little, so sweet. It was my job to keep her safe and I failed. I would go home every night and do it all over again until she came home with us. Every day, a little piece of me was dying inside because of the guilt.

The day we brought her home I was a nervous wreck. This tiny little human had already been through enough and I didn't want to hurt her again. I really didn't. *But the thing about addiction is that it lingers until you do something to really change your mindset.* I thought I was ready for this. I thought I would change. I thought I could be this tiny little baby's mommy. *I thought wrong.*

Forgiving yourself truly gives you a chance at life.

CHAPTER 7

HEROIN, TAKE TWO

We took it slow on the way home because we didn't want to harm her. *Now I worry about harming her?.....sheesh.* She was the sweetest little baby and had the cutest little pie face. After the detox, she was fine. I thank God all the time that nothing worse happened to her. Being this little sweeties' mom was something I knew little about. So, I winged it and took it day by day. My Mama loved Destiny and was a big help to us. I think it was kind of a "do-over" for her.

Fortunately, Stewart and I were still together which was very helpful but we were just kids ourselves and it was hard.

Every day, we packed her up and lugged her to the methadone clinic with us. All of the other patients loved seeing her and thought she was so precious. Day in and day out at the clinic became her life as well. We finally got a car but I wrecked it because the methadone dose they had me on was too high. Destiny was in the car when I had the wreck but we were both okay. The next day at the clinic, I was tapered down to a lower dose. I was a great patient. I went to my groups, did my acupuncture, talked to my counselor, and lied through my teeth. *Just because I was on methadone, didn't mean I couldn't smoke weed, take benzos, or drink alcohol, right?* And of course, I did all of those. The mindset I had was that if I had to be on methadone, I was still going to use other drugs because I thought I would be fine. However, it was very dangerous mixing all those drugs but I thought I was invincible. I passed all my drug tests by bringing in "clean" pee for all my tests from a big stash of it that I saved before I started using again. I would warm it up before I went to the clinic. I did this for two years...*two freaking years!* Luckily, I got away with it and I got to keep my daughter.

About a week after graduating from the methadone clinic, Stewart was nodding out in the chair at home. Right away, I knew he was back on heroin. I just knew it. I walked down the hall of our home and looked down. There it was...aluminum foil filled with heroin, my true love. At first, I was pissed and hid it from him. Then, I went into the bathroom, looked at it in my hand, and it went right up my nose. All of the feelings rushed through my body...guilt, love, shame, warmth, comfort, and anger. There I was after two years of methadone, right back on heroin. *Addiction is a BEAST!*

Slowly my life returned right back to where I was before I had Destiny, but now she was in the middle of it. *What a nightmare!* This beautiful little baby was stuck in our chaos. I thought about using every now and then, but that doesn't work with heroin, your body needs it every day. *It sucks you in like the devil.* In my heart, I wanted to be this little girl's mom, but my mind was messed up. You would think after all the hell I had been through that I could stop using and it was that easy. *WRONG!* It was not easy, especially with opiates. After I started using again, the shame and guilt entered my soul like fireworks. At first, it didn't seem as bad. But then I started lying again to friends and family to cover it up. *That was exhausting!* If our families knew we were using again, they would have tried to take Destiny from us. They should have.

Unfortunately, we were experts at being fake. Things changed between Stewart and I as well. We kept things from one another because we each wanted our own supply of drugs. We lived day by day not knowing what was going to happen to us. Living with his stepdad didn't last too long because they were always fighting. Eventually, we left and went to live with my Mama. Even though Destiny was definitely loved, she was part of a very unhealthy lifestyle.

My relationship with my Mama was toxic and now there is a baby in the mix which made it worse. Not to mention, living in my childhood home brought back a lot of negative vibes for me. *The good thing about being on heroin...I could push those negative vibes out of my head.* My Mama decided to sell our home and we all had to move into an apartment. We lived in an upstairs apartment and she was in hers, downstairs. It wasn't that great of a place, but she paid for it with the money she got from the sale of the house so how could I complain. *I thought this would change us. I thought we would stop using. I thought we could be a cute little family without drugs being involved. Once again, I thought wrong.* I was great at wishful thinking. Well, I wished, but I didn't think that much.

We made a few friends in the apartment building...those that used heroin with us of course. In order to function each day, we needed to use it. I wanted out of this life. Finally, I found employment at a company that sells land. It was a job with a steady income. The staff were really cool and I quickly learned who I could trust. I showed up, did my job, and went home to the chaos. Even though this job made me feel like I had a purpose, my addiction was still more important. To top it off, getting a regular paycheck wasn't enough because we blew through it each and every payday. So my solution was to go to every payday loan place I could find. At least five of them lent me money but with every paycheck, I had to pay it back so that I could borrow more. It was a vicious cycle. And when that didn't work, we became criminals.

During my addiction, I hurt people in many ways, and stealing was definitely one of them. *When you are in the grip of addiction, you don't let anyone or anything stand in the way of getting drugs.* Anything and everything we could possibly pawn, we did. With Destiny in tow, we kept her smiling with a Happy Meal and a toy. But in this drug-induced lifestyle, I started to hate myself even more than before. Not to mention, I was unfaithful to him...her father...my boyfriend. I manipulated other men to get what I needed. The things I did sucked the soul right out of me. It reached the point where I couldn't take care of Destiny anymore. Shit, I could barely take care of myself. Living off of McDonald's drive-thru was not ideal nutrition for a four-year-old.

My family began recognizing my old behaviors. There are only so many change jars and DVDs that can go missing from one house. They knew it was me taking them. This time my Deddy and sisters showed up at my apartment to confront me. We were trapped like rats. Being in a third-floor apartment, there was nowhere to run. It was somewhat of an intervention minus the TV crew and the heartfelt letters. They basically told me to get my shit together or they were taking Destiny.

Reluctantly, I agreed to go to treatment. *Well, my idea was to do a rapid detox with a local doctor and maybe treatment.* I was so embarrassed to tell my job. My boss told me to go to the 28-Day program and that my position would be there for me when I got back. My parents took me to a doctor that I had been to years earlier for my addiction. In the past this didn't work but this time, it was a different procedure. I was given all these meds to detox for days and then on the last day they were going to flush my system. During the detox, I was using heroin that Stewart was sneaking me and benzos. *That was a HORRIBLE idea. I could have died.* Again, my addiction took over everything decent in me. My Mama had my daughter, my Deddy and Derby were trying to detox me, Stewart was still using, and I was a nutcase. I went as far as to hide the detox pills so I didn't have to take them. On the last day at the doctor when they flushed my system, I went into immediate withdrawal.

My brain remembers bits and pieces like movie clips. I tried to steal my parent's *(Deddy and Derby are now married)* car but my Deddy held me down. I was a raging lunatic trying to jump out of the car. They had to hold the seat belt to keep it in the buckle. I am sure they wanted to knock me out. Something happened chemically in my poor lil' brain. The next thing I knew, I woke up a couple of days later in a recovery treatment program in Winchester, VA. I was told that I was a human zombie when I got there, just like one of my favorite shows, *The Walking Dead*. My parents packed my ass up, took me there, and left me. *Now in hindsight, I get it. I am very grateful for all that they tried to do to save my life.* At the moment though, I WAS PISSED. *No more drugs? What is the treatment? Can I escape? Can I lie? Will I ever be a normal human?*

Value your family, they will be there until the end.

CHAPTER 8

FALLING IN LUST

After waking up in rehab, my mind was very unclear. I took a shower, threw on some eyeliner, and walked out of this little room under the stairs. I felt like I was a giant in a dollhouse. It was so random and weird. The staff filled me in on what happened two days prior to me feeling like I was in *Honey, I Shrunk The Kids.* They informed me nicely that when I came in I was a whack job. Something chemically happened in my brain because of the heroin, detox drugs, and the medicine that was given to me on the way to this place. I peed myself, laughed a lot, cussed a lot, and don't remember ANY of it. And the reason I was in this tiny room, was because originally they put me in a bunk bed and I fell off the top bunk. Why I was on the top, I have no clue.

Clearly, I was out of my mind. For safety purposes, the right choice was to hide me under the stairs. While I was in the TV room drooling all over myself and nodding out, there was a guy in there that threw balls of trash at me and thought it was funny because I had no idea they were hitting me. *He was a real winner.* As I walked around introducing myself, the other residents were all like, "We met two days ago." *I was a zombie, give me a freaking break.*

It was the first time in thirteen years that I was semi-drug-free because I was still on detox meds. Slowly, I started to open up a tad and made a couple of friends. With my mind getting a little clearer, I started talking about my relationship with Stewart and got lots of advice from people. Now in this program, I was supposed to focus on me and only me. I called Stewart from the payphone at the rehab and broke up with him. I was done; I was tired; I was free. *Well, for like a day or so.*

Then one day, I walked outside to smoke a cig and there he was...my new victim, his name was Adam *(the one that threw the balls of trash at me)*. Watching him play basketball made me fall in lust immediately. He was into sports, cute, tall, and in rehab. *WINNER!!!* We flirted, laughed and I felt happy again, whatever "happy" is supposed to feel like. Unfortunately, I still didn't know who the hell I was, so I just pretended to be something I thought he would like. All of my life, I lied. *Well, let's call it over embellishing the truth. Who am I kidding? I was a straight up liar.* We lived under the same roof at this place which is never a good combination in a rehab setting. Yes, we snuck around any chance we could to give each other smooches. We went to many of the same 12-Step meetings and groups. *It was a cute little rehab romance!*

My family brought my daughter to see me on the week-ends. It was the first time completely drug-free that I spent with her. My heart was loving it, but my mind would sabo-tage all of it. The feelings of shame, guilt, and hatred for myself crept in. Seeing her cry when it was time for her to leave, crushed me. *Like, an elephant on my chest...crush.* But, I needed to try to get better for her and I really tried this time.

This place taught me things about myself and finally, I was open to change. At least, I thought I was.

After my twenty-eight days, I headed back to Richmond. My apartment, job, car, and kid were all handed back to me. To say I was overwhelmed was an understatement. This was the first time I was drug-free. No detox meds, no heroin, no alcohol, no weed, but I did have my cigs. Going back to work was awkward. I lied and stole from my place of work. I said and did things that I wasn't proud of. But every day, I kept pushing through; did my job; picked up my daughter from daycare; and went home. This was it, this was the life I thought I may have one day.

The weekend I came home, Adam drove from Winchester to see me. He had to stay in Winchester because he had a lot of open criminal charges over his head. He ended up living in a recovery house there for a couple more months. We drove back and forth to see one another. The back and forth became exhausting, but I was in lust. I continued to go to 12-Step meetings and my new sponsor who was younger than me was super cool. After two months, Adam asked to move in with me. I ran the idea past my sponsor and she said that it wasn't a great idea. *Do you know what I heard? DO IT!*

So in moved Adam, the man *I* met in rehab from West Virginia to live with me and Destiny. I felt happy, however, I never really knew what true happiness was. He was great with Destiny and we became a little family. We both went to meetings but after a month or so, he stopped going. So I thought...*why should I have to keep going? I am sure you can guess what happened next.* I started with weed again and he rolled me some beautiful blunts to smoke after work. Since he was not able to join me in smoking due to some unfinished court business where he would be drug tested, I decided to smoke them in front of him. I figured he could get a contact buzz and not fail a drug test. After all his court stuff was over, we both started drinking and smoking weed together. We went to a *Wailers* concert and we were drunk before we even walked in. He was puking at the car so I left his ass to go dance in the concert. While I was flinging all around and not having a care in the world, suddenly someone came up to me. It was my sponsor from my 12-step recovery meetings. *Run, hide, too late...* At that point, I knew I was busted and I knew I wouldn't go back to the meetings anymore. *Damn it, here I go again.* Within a week, I started to mix the alcohol with benzos. *Days...I am talking about days gone... missing from my life.*

There was a time before all of this when I took a bunch of benzos to cope with life. I happened to be at a business event and literally woke up the next day in one of the boss's beds. The sad thing is that I remember nothing. *Even sadder...is if I was out of my mind, why would he take advantage of me? All I could think about was: A. running, B. he is going to find a way to fire me, and C. he is married. What an asshole. Take it from me, if you aren't prescribed benzos or are not taking them like you are supposed to...DON'T DO IT! For me, they are evil.*

One of my friends from work had to get the landlord to let her into my apartment because I didn't show up for days. I was fired from my job and didn't know what to do. Adam was working so that was helpful. **And then, we decided to start using heroin together.**

First, we had to search out less than desirable neighborhoods to find it. *Everything happened so fast!* On the outside, we tried to keep up appearances but I know I was looking rough and thought no one noticed. And, getting a new job wasn't really part of my plan. I found some temp work here and there, but it wasn't for me. If I could lie or panhandle, I preferred to do that. Then my hurricane of lies to my family started all over again but we got money from them. And at the time, that is all that mattered. This year of using drugs was the worst out of all fourteen years of my addiction. *All I did was shoot heroin.* There was something so different from shooting heroin than sniffing it. The warmth traveling through your veins and the immediate nodding off were what I craved. There was nothing like it. Trying to get needles from pharmacies was complicated so we used the same ones over and over. It sucked.

And there was my precious Destiny stuck in the middle. Young enough not to know what was going on, but old enough to remember a few things. I put her in danger constantly by committing felonies with her in the back seat. If I had been caught and punished for these crimes I would probably still be in prison today. *There was that guardian angel again making sure I didn't go to the big house.*

One time, I locked myself in the bathroom trying to hit my vein with a needle and Destiny was outside in the hall crying because she wanted to play. In heroin addiction, there is no playing; there is no laughing; there is no having fun with your daughter, at least not while you are dopesick. Even though I was on heroin, I thought I could fulfill my "being a mom" duties except when I was dopesick. Otherwise, I thought I was on point in my efforts. Every day I would try hard, yet heroin seemed to be more important to me. Guilt overtook my soul and I just couldn't be her mom anymore. I took her downstairs to my Mama and left her there. The pain that caused me was immeasurable. Feeling worthless, I just wanted to die and let her live a life without me. My addiction didn't care that I couldn't be a mother, it was screaming more, more, more.

For months, I popped over to my Mama's to steal money

or food, and seeing Destiny broke my heart. I used more heroin to cover up my pain. This was a whole new level of "mom guilt". I felt like a piece of shit; I hated myself; I didn't want to be here, but I just kept repeating the same pattern. And so, it was back to panhandling for me. My role in the relationship with Adam was to bring in as much money as I could. I even went as far as to pawn Destiny's things like her Dora the Explorer television set. *Poor Dora.*

One night after we committed a very intense crime, Adam almost overdosed. He did entirely too much heroin. That particular night between looking out the window to see if cops were coming and putting ice on his privates I couldn't even feel my high. It was one of the scariest nights of my life. He survived and we didn't get arrested. *Let's keep this train moving then.*

God puts people in our lives for a reason, it is up to you to see why.

CHAPTER 9

WELCOME TO THE MCSHIN FOUNDATION

Every day I told Adam, "Today is the last day we are using." This went on for months with no end in sight. After we bought drugs, the only food I could afford were those Little Debbie Zebra Cakes that sell for $0.25. *I have not eaten a SINGLE Zebra Cake since I have been in recovery.* Eventually, we sold everything in our apartment and ran out of lies to tell to our parents. We were completely broke.

That was it, lying to my Deddy was over, no more making up stories that I needed $20 for a broken car part. I was finally able to tell him that I would rather die than be dopesick. He responded, "Okay." I was pissed off by his reaction, but I knew something had to change. My family had finally given up on me, rightfully so.

However, Derby showed up at our apartment and told me to get off my ass. She wanted me to go meet one of her friends that had a non-profit that helped those with addiction. I wasn't going to attempt to meet him while I was dopesick. After I scrounged up money, I bought heroin. And then, I went to meet this friend of hers. Our first meeting was a blur because I was high. He told me he could get me a detox doctor's info and I could get withdrawal meds. That was enough to get me to come back the next day but there was a hiccup in the process of getting the detox medication. So, I used heroin in the recovery house that night. The next day, Adam moved into the recovery house for men. While in one of our group meetings, he got my attention and said he could get $30. I pretended that I was going to smoke but instead I hauled ass down the road to get my Jeep. Nothing mattered to me but that $30. I scooped Adam up and we left for a few days. It was complete misery and I wanted detox meds. I called the founder of the recovery organization, John Shinholser, and asked to come back. Withdrawing badly, I had to see the doctor before I could return to the recovery house.

I was hopeful that this doctor was going to make me feel better. He was my new best friend. The paperwork was done; questions were answered; and I was ready for my meds. When he handed them to me, all of a sudden I had the thought that this wasn't going to work. I had tried to detox and failed at it miserably in the past. My plan was to pretend to take the meds in front of him and leave with the bottle to take home. This way, Adam and I could detox together but God had different plans for me. After I took the meds out of my mouth when the doctor wasn't looking, they started melting in my hand. Then something happened that I didn't expect, he said "Okay, now we sit here for four hours together." *FOUR FREAKING HOURS? How in the hell was I going to sit there being sick as shit and the meds just chilling in my hand?* I looked up to God, looked at the meds, and then said, "F" it while putting the meds back in my mouth. **That was May 27, 2007, and I haven't used alcohol or drugs since that day...**a very special day for me, hopefully forever.*

After I started to feel better, I went back to our apartment that we were supposedly evicted from (they never came to kick us out) and Adam was there, waiting. As I was telling him everything that just happened, it made me think. *Maybe I could go back to that recovery house? Maybe my life can change?* I called John and he said, "Sure, come on back." The next day, I moved into The McShin Foundation. I didn't know it then, but this place would literally save my life.

Because I was a super stubborn woman, I thought I would only live there a week or so while taking my detox meds. Before I went to live there, regular, normal human things like eating and showering were things that I wasn't really doing much of. Derby brought me a carton of Marlboro Lights, gave me gift cards to Arby's, and hand-delivered my detox meds to me every day. She was a saint and I am forever grateful to her for not giving up on me. Something happened after that first week, it was that good feeling of not using heroin all day, every day.

What is this feeling? Can I do this every day?

I didn't know the answers, but I kept going to bed drug-free and waking up drug-free every morning. On the front porch of that recovery house, I had to break up with Adam. It sucked and I know it hurt him but I had to figure out why the hell I couldn't stop using drugs. He went to another recovery apartment somewhere else and I walked back into my new home. McShin was exactly what I needed even though I wasn't exactly willing to accept that.

The McShin Foundation is a recovery community organization designed to help those with addiction. There are a lot of rules and guidelines you have to live by while in the housing. Of course, I didn't like it, obviously. *Insert eye roll here :)* Most days I whined, cried, cussed, and bitched about the rules as well as not being able to use daily. *I used drugs for fourteen years!!!* There was no female staff, just John and two other men. That was annoying in itself, but I listened for the most part and didn't leave. Rules were broken; lies were told for a few weeks; but drugs were not used. The female recovery community adopted me since there were no female staff members. There was a female volunteer who would hang out sometimes at the recovery center, named Kelli. She would listen to me, co-sign my bullshit, and then we would smoke cigs. She is one of my closest friends to this day. Being drug-free was foreign to me, but the best part was not being dopesick and not having to worry every few hours about how I was going to get money. That life was EXHAUSTING! After a couple of weeks, a man named Daniel hired me to help clean houses and do yard work for his small business. I jumped on the opportunity but complained a lot. In early recovery with no drugs to help cope with my feelings, I bitched about everything. *It is very hard to just stop using drugs after being on them for so long and then dealing with real life.*

Eventually, I stopped complaining and accepted my situation. My life was slowly, like a very slow turtle pace, getting better. The biggest thing Daniel gave me was hope when he asked me to be a nanny for his one-year-old son. *I felt less than...how could I take care of someone else's kid and I couldn't even take care of my own?* That hit my heart hard! I am eternally grateful to him and his wife, McKenzie, for taking a chance on me. This is what recovery is about, hope dealing.

Days turned into weeks and weeks turned into months. The recovery house was cool and I got to meet some interesting people who were like me. I didn't know how to cope with other people's personalities and no drugs, so that sucked. Being early in recovery was hard enough, but I was thrown in with a bunch of other women going through the same thing. *Look Out!* Recovery was beautiful at times, but sharing two bathrooms with ten women going through all kinds of feelings made the tension in that space very high. *But at least we were not high!* These women were from all walks of life, a couple are still my friends today. Recovery house life isn't simple, but it was worth every second.

Here I was literally starting a life from scratch at twenty-six years old. Just a couple trash bags full of clothes, a beat up Jeep Cherokee, and some photo albums is all I had. My life needed to change, and I knew it was going to be hard. I learned early in recovery that if I don't use drugs or alcohol, I can handle anything. Though I truly believe that, there is so much more to recovery that I had to learn throughout this journey in order to survive. *So, this is it...recovery.* Out of all the years I tried to stop using, a recovery organization, a ten-day opiate detox, and a 12-Step program were what I needed to truly learn how to heal and live without drugs.

During my stay at McShin, I didn't have the opportunity to see Destiny very often. But one special morning, I went to my Mama's and put Destiny on the school bus for her first day of school. Seeing her cute little pie face smiling with missing teeth, her cute little glasses, and her short little haircut meant the world to me. I will never ever forget that day. This is actually one memory that plays in my mind like it was yesterday. So many emotions flowed through me...joy, sadness, guilt, and gratefulness. Even though I was living in a recovery house and did not have much of anything, I still had gratitude that I could be there with her for that special moment without being high. I got in my beat up Jeep and cried all the way to work. While I sobbed in my Jeep, I told myself...*one day, one day we would have a home where I would be able to get her on and off the school bus from our very own driveway.*

After about four months into my recovery process, I

slowly started dating Adam again. Truthfully, I didn't know if I wanted to be with him, but it just felt right. Four months isn't really that long of a time period, and I felt like my brain was barely human. Now, we actually had money to go on dates. *Holla!* It was awkward at first because we used drugs together. The trauma from that was still so fresh. Taking it slow was what I needed and I made that clear to him. Then, I had to tell my Deddy. I wanted to run and hide forever. Deddy didn't like any man that did drugs with me because he always blamed my drug use on the man. I knew he wasn't going to be cool with Adam and I dating again. Our conversation was heated and I tried to reassure him that it would be different this time, but I didn't bring Adam around him for quite a while. *Was four months long enough to be on my own, without a man?* I didn't know. But I knew that I needed every single minute of those four months to prove that I could look in a mirror and like what I saw, a little. *Like a tiny sparkle.*

Living at McShin and seeing my life slowly change was a miracle. The time came for me to get Destiny back and to be her mother for real. I was so scared, I wanted to puke. My older sister offered for Destiny and I to live with her until I saved enough money to get my own place. That was super cool of her and I am forever grateful. Now, it was time to be a full-time mommy. *How will I do this? Will I be good enough for her? Will I harm her again? Will I be okay? Will she be okay?*

The only thing I could do was try. I left McShin; got Destiny from my Mama's; moved into my sister's apartment; and quit smoking cigs. I am eternally grateful that my Mama stepped in to fill a role I could not, but it was time for me to do this myself. After leaving the recovery house, I started working at McShin. The goal was to help the women since there were no other female staff. My administrative skills from the past helped me do the job and I enjoyed helping the women. Working both at McShin and for Daniel kept the bills paid. Coming into recovery, I was about $40K in debt. Slowly, I started paying back that debt. I didn't have much to spare back then because I was a single mother trying to make it. Stewart didn't contribute because he was in jail. *To all the single Mama's out there working their asses off to support their kids with no baby daddy help....I send you a HUGE hug. It is hard, but I did it, and so can you!*

Sometimes we have to just throw up our hands and give up, rest, and just breathe.

CHAPTER 10

HUMAN CONFLICTS

Being a mom? Hmm...what does that even mean? What is she going to wear? How am I going to pay for things she wants? How do I handle misbehavior? Do I give her everything? Do I punish her? What the hell DO I DO??? I didn't know because I was never really taught how to be a mother. Every day was a challenge. The only thing I knew how to do was show up and be there for her everyday as I was learning how to be a mom. Most days, I was winging it and I prayed a lot! Knowing there would be a ton of healing to do, gave me anxiety. My addiction put this little girl through hell, and now I had to learn how to help her through it. *IT WAS HARD.* The guilt I had overtook me some days so I gave her any toy I could afford. *Then there were days when I was like WTF, who is this child? And why is she such a "meanie pants"?*

I decided to use a reward calendar for her to earn things. When that phase was over, I tried something else, and then something else, and then something else. Obviously, I was a single mom and didn't know what the heck I was doing. My sisters helped the best they could, but they didn't have any kids of their own. Destiny went with me to meetings every night. We threw on her head phones and she watched something or played a game on her tablet. *I needed those meetings. I didn't want to use drugs again. I didn't want to ruin my relationship with her again.*

Recovery is all about communication. Well, I got a big fat "F" in my early years of recovery. Trying to figure out who the hell I am, hold a job, go to 12-Step meetings, be a mom, have a boyfriend, and show up for life was a lot to handle. This freaked me out because the last time I had so many responsibilities at once, I used heroin. Consistently, something was always out of balance. I did my best but got overwhelmed when I couldn't. Having great friends, like Rachel, helped me. She always had the right thing to say, especially when I went through some "cray, cray" situations. While I was using, I never knew what true friendship was but recovery taught me that it is possible. *Rachel to this day is a calming presence in my life. I know I wouldn't be writing this book today if it wasn't for her friendship all these years as well as her guidance in my recovery.*

Because I started using drugs at a young age, I didn't have such a "hot" childhood. My communication skills were made up of telling lies or running away from situations. Now, it felt super weird having drug-free relationships. I had to learn how to use my words and express my feelings. *PUKE!* It was hard, especially with Adam. I didn't know who the hell I was, let alone how I was going to grow in a relationship with a man. But, I was willing to learn how to.

Because I had such low self-esteem and body image issues that had always created an inner conflict for me, I didn't feel 100% comfortable with him. *Thank God there is always work you can do to help with that mess in your soul.*

There was a free Hepatitis C screening at McShin that I decided to take part in because everyone else was doing it.

When I got the phone call regarding the results, *guess what….we have a winner…*the woman on the other end said, "You have tested positive." All I knew was that it was an illness, and my next thought was that I was going to die. *Literally, THE NEXT THOUGHT.* Of course, I panicked and called Rachel. She suggested seeing a medical professional. I did but during this time there was only one treatment for Hep C and I was not going to do it. This medicine made you sick, like dopesick. *Nope. I never want to have that feeling again…never!* I left the appointment, did some research, and was super careful after that. There was no way to find out how I transmitted it, but I know it was from those dirty needles I used every day.

Moving forward was all I could do at that moment. I was celebrating a year in recovery and it felt like a freaking miracle. There was a time when I couldn't have imagined celebrating a week, let alone a whole year. Adam wanted to take the next step in our relationship and move in together with me and Destiny. At first, I was hesitant because of our past but we both had one year in recovery. *So I said, "Let's do it!"*

Our first apartment was precious and it was completely ours. *Well, we rented.* Destiny had her own room and she loved it. My relationship with Destiny was healing each day and I was actually an okay mom. None of her new toys or gift cards were stolen by me; she had food to eat; she had a safe place to live; and we weren't putting her in danger anymore. *That was a win.*

Finally, life was pretty good. Adam and I started playing football in a co-ed league with a bunch of our friends and my sister. Even Deddy and Derby played a season. We loved it! Our friends were amazing and it was so fun to be a part of a cool team. When I played, it brought back my love of football from those Sundays at Nannie's and watching it on television with my Deddy. During these games, I realized how competitive I was and some days it wasn't so pretty. Again, I saw how I needed help with communication. But for the most part, being on that field and making plays is something I still treasure.

With Adam and I moving forward, there came another conflict for me. We discussed having a baby but I was very hesitant. Being diagnosed with Hep C meant that I might transfer it to my baby upon delivery. Because I never wanted to put another child in danger, I told Adam that I wasn't going to have any more kids. There was so much trauma instilled in me from my pregnancy with Destiny, I was scared. His heart was broken and with that came a lot of fighting because we were on two different pages in our relationship. I know he didn't fully understand how I felt. Plus, I was only about one and a half years drug-free and I was getting used to being Destiny's mother. *I could barely afford to do that well.* Adam wanted a child. I know in his deepest dreams he wanted a boy because of sports, sports, and more sports. But he wouldn't have to live with giving a precious little baby a disease, I would. We took a little break from one another, like two days. *And it wasn't no "Ross and Rachel" break!* After talking it over with our friends, we started to communicate much better with one another about the situation. After two days, he came back home. We made up, had sex, and that night our son was conceived. *God has a plan for everyone.* It was Christmastime when I took that pregnancy test. *Merry Christmas to us!* I had many feelings rush over me while sitting in my bathroom looking at that stick. *Is this real? I am going to puke. How am I going to do this? What should I do?* It felt like a TV show but instead, it was my reality. *This was not The Real Housewives of NY (my fave), this was Honesty*

Liller's life. No cameras, no producers, just me and a test that changed my life.

I walked out to the living room where Adam and Destiny were wrapping Christmas presents. I told Adam to look on the counter in the bathroom. He came out with the biggest smile I have ever seen. This was it. I was pregnant and Destiny was going to be a big sister. Of course, she was the first one we told and she was so excited. Then came the baby showers with lots of family and friends. And food, there was so much food! This pregnancy was completely different because I was not using drugs. So I got big, like VERY big. In the doctor's office, when we found out we were having a baby boy, Adam jumped out of the chair and screamed. That was a wrap, one boy, one girl. We were going to be DONE after this angel came out of me and graced us with his presence. *Still in the back of my mind the whole time, am I going to get this sweet boy sick? Is the stress of this going to make me want to use drugs again? Can I handle two children? Am I doing this correctly?*

I didn't have the answers to any of those questions. All I knew was to take care of myself, not use drugs, and communicate my feelings as best I could. It was very, very hard but I did it.

During my pregnancy, my whole family took a trip to the mountains and I couldn't do much but eat. One night, we were playing charades which was one of our favorite things to do as a family. Adam was up and moving all around like a weirdo. Our family is a very loud family so we were all screaming trying to figure out what the hell he was doing. When the time was up, I was pissed because his performance sucked. I blurted out, "What the hell was that?" and then, he threw the paper in my lap with the answer on it. I opened it and it said, "Will you marry me?" I cried. He was bent down on one knee with a ring and asked me himself in front of my whole family. I said, "No way…..haha, just kidding." I said, "Yes!" And everyone was so happy for us! *Maybe this life is going to be totally amazing?* I was never the girl that wanted to get married even as a child because I thought marriage was hard and angry. As a young adult I was so focused on drugs, marriage was the last thing on my mind. My parent's marriage wasn't one to admire, so I was torn about actually doing it myself. *But, maybe, just maybe this will be great and we could do this.*

We all need to do the best with what we got one day at a time.

CHAPTER 11

MOMMY'S LIL' SWEETIE

It was a hot July day when I went to my OB/GYN for a check-up. Our sweet little boy was coming into our lives very soon...maybe even sooner than we had thought. I had high blood pressure so they admitted me into the hospital. I felt like I was as big as a house! My feet were swollen like I had been stung by 100 bees, and I was scared. Adam rushed to the hospital to be by my side. My doctor told me we could wait to see if I would have contractions or I could have a C-Section. *Okay, I am huge, hungry, and they told me I could only eat ice chips until our son was born. Nope! Let's have the C-Section.* There was a complication when they tried to get him out of my belly, he was stuck. Well of course he was, I have a small frame and he was 9.5 lbs! I heard some squishy noises and then there he was sounding like a little lamb. My whole body was overwhelmed with emotion as I saw our lil' Wyatt (AKA Mommy's Lil' Sweetie). His round little perfect face looked up at me and I melted. *I thought...today I have met my second and last child.* Watching Destiny's eyes light up when she met him made my whole world stop.

Looking at the two of them together, I knew that was why

I am here. This was the reason why I didn't lose my life while using, and why I will hopefully never use drugs again. Seeing Adam with both of our kids was priceless. Even though he met Destiny when she was four, he stepped in to be her father, he will always be her father.

Shortly after bringing Wyatt home, we moved out of our apartment and got a small rental house. There wasn't much income between the two of us, but this house was perfect. Our kids had their own rooms which was very important to me. Before long, the day came for me to become Mrs. Liller. Our kids, closest friends, and family were all a part of this beautiful day. It all flew by so quickly, but I was surrounded by everyone that loved me and Adam.

There I was married, a mom of two, working at a job I loved, and helping others. It was a dream I never even knew I had. And the best part...Wyatt didn't get Hepatitis C. *What a relief! I actually cured my Hep C with medication a couple years ago! YAY!* Going through all of the emotional ups and downs for almost two years was not fun, but God had a plan for all of us. My husband brought home our first family doggie, Jax. He was a mixed pitbull that we adopted from the shelter. Having a dog in our home really completed our family. Wyatt was one year old and would play with him all the time. Jax was the best dog.

We recently lost Jax to diabetes and it has been one of the hardest things to heal from. Dogs are family and losing a family member sucks!

After having Wyatt, my body image issues created a lot of negative feelings in my brain. I gained a lot of weight during my pregnancy and for someone who already hated her body, having a baby made it worse. With so many insecurities, I was battling fears that weren't even real. Good thing I had so many strong, positive women in my life that helped me through this. Rachel would always take the time to listen to me, and listen to the negative things I thought about myself while she also gave me positive motivation. I was carrying around so much pain from childhood and trauma from using drugs. I needed to heal. The women I have in my life are so important to me. *You have to let that shit out or it will eat you alive. My friends let me do that; they don't judge; and they love me for who I am.*

Rachel has been there from day one on this journey with me and she knows most of my insane thoughts. *In order for me to continue to grow as a person, I needed to hang out with other women that are living a life in recovery. Without them, I don't know where I would be. And God knows, I needed them when I found out that Adam was using heroin yet again.*

Everything was going so well, and then my whole world came crashing down around me. There were days when I was suspicious and I didn't want to believe it. Then one night, I just knew and I went into an immediate rage. He tried to deny it for like five seconds but he knew he was busted. I found heroin in the house and I knew it wasn't mine. Just the sight of that heroin was like tourture. Emotions exploded through my entire mind and body. I cried and yelled, then cried and yelled some more all while I was trying to not wake up the kids. The next morning he asked for my help and I told him to call John at McShin. My heart was broken. I thought we would be in recovery forever together. John helped him of course because that is what John does. This was a major crack in our marriage. There was no way that I could be the one to save him. I had to protect our children and I had to protect myself. Our children needed me and I couldn't throw away all of my hard work over the past five years. A part of me was really jealous too. Being addicted to heroin for so many years doesn't ever leave your mind totally. *Why does he get to get high? Why can't I? Can I? Wait, Can I? No, I will not.*

He started his recovery path over and worked very hard at it which led to the beginning of our healing. After his use, I was thinking about what could be wrong with me or our life together. *Why would he use? Was it me? Was it our family?* But the thing is, people have a recurrence of use sometimes and they just need to learn how to live again without drugs. It is their shit, not yours. I thank God that Adam turned it around so quickly and hasn't used again since that day, almost nine years ago. *Prayer works. Whether you believe in God or spirits or whatever, try some form of prayer. This can just be talking to the sky, writing in a journal, or sitting in silence. These things have helped me so many times I can't even count.*

Our kids have always been around people in recovery. They practically grew up at McShin. They got to see first hand how to help people and have experienced lots of love while hearing lots of "F" bombs. *It is better than taking them around drug dealers like I did with Destiny when she was young.* Being a parent is the hardest thing I will ever do. I like to call myself a "real model" to my children, meaning we keep it real in our house. I feel like being a role model is for the individual. A real model is a way to live with how you treat people, how you forgive, how you grow, and how you love.

Situations arose with Destiny as a tween and I was like *WTF*. The cool thing was that we were able to talk about them openly. That is something that I didn't have as a kid. I was never really taught how to express my feelings. There were no "sex" or "drug" talks in my household. Adam and I chose to raise our children differently than the way both of us were raised. This was HARD AS CRAP! Of course we made mistakes but we were doing the best we could day to day. Our kids were happy and got everything they needed. They didn't always get what they wanted earlier in life because Adam and I just didn't have the funds. I was still paying off my old debt and we didn't make that much at our jobs. Our kids seemed okay with that because we would talk to them about it when they wanted something boujee. My response to them was always, "I am healing families and saving lives, that is better than tons of money."

As the years went by at McShin, the company had so much growth. The need was huge because many more people were addicted and with growth always comes challenges. There was lots of work to be done to help those like me and McShin was a pioneer on how to do it. I started traveling a lot to help other states advocate for change as well as start their own RCO (Recovery Community Organization). Back then, McShin had very little staff which meant I was working a lot trying to do the best job I could. However, it took away from my family life. I didn't really see it at the time, but I was stressed and tension was high at home. Sometimes, I even lost focus on my recovery. Having an addictive brain, there is always more to do. *Helping more and more, can bite you in the ass.*

I loved my job and I loved helping people but I just didn't know how to balance everything in my life. Everything came to a screeching halt one day when I opened my husband's computer to google something. And there, right in front of me were messages to another woman on Facebook. I read them; my heart pounded through my chest; I shut the computer; and ran to call Rachel. I immediately cried my eyes out to her on the phone. Rage couldn't touch what I was feeling. Rachel helped by calming me down. John talked me out of killing Adam. And Carol, John's wife, told me ways to prepare myself if there was a divorce. *I have the coolest friends.*

One of my dearest friends, Megan, came over to hang out with the kids so Adam and I could talk outside at our patio table. There wasn't much talking; instead there was yelling; and there were a lot of "F" bombs coming from me. I kept saying, "I don't understand." Emotions soared through my veins just like heroin used to. At first, I thought our life together was over and that I would hate him forever. All I truly knew was that I couldn't use and I couldn't kill him because I really didn't want to go to jail. *This time in my life was gut wrenching. Do all relationships end this way? It is what I have known for most of my life, lies, cheating, and misery.* Although it was just a few messages to an old girl-friend from his past, it still cut like a knife in my heart. *Would I always wonder if it would happen again?* I had to do a lot of soul work with Rachel to be able to forgive him and also to be able to see my part in it as well. That situation, even though it was ugly, became something beautiful for our marriage. We started to have raw and real conversations that had been held back for years. Neither one of us really knew how to talk about feelings, our sex life, and how we were truly doing in our souls. But, this helped us. *I adore this man today. And sometimes, relationships have some mountains you need to climb in order to see the sunshine.*

However, because this happened with Adam and I have body image issues, I started to get obsessed with running. The stress about needing to workout and run, opposed to me really wanting to, made me calculate my week out by when I could get a run in. I was literally obsessed. Still carrying a lot of baby weight from my pregnancy with Wyatt, I thought if I looked better then Adam would never look at another woman again. *I know, I know, but this is my story.* My fears and insecurities overtook me. My behaviors at home and at work weren't exactly nice. *Not liking what you look like or how you feel about yourself hurts those around you too. I thought to myself...Girl, you got a lot of work to do.*

Marriage is like hiking a mountain and it is worth every bit of happiness when you get to see that amazing view.

CHAPTER 12
WOMEN RULE

Healing is a process and I know for me that process was life-changing.

Finally, our marriage was thriving and our life was getting much better. Then John told me that he would like to name me CEO of McShin. I was beyond honored and was speechless which is really rare. *What does being a CEO even mean? I didn't do a day in college. Can I be a CEO? Am I smart enough? Will I fail? Will I suck?* My self-esteem still wasn't the greatest during this time in my life, so I second-guessed myself often. But I knew there, I would be a female CEO of a respected non-profit organization. (#winning) Having a title meant that there were more expectations placed on me, expectations that I didn't know I could fulfill. *But I tried, and tried again.* It helped that I had other female leaders in my network that mentored me like John's wife, Carol McDaid. She continues to teach me how to have a voice and never give up.

I use my story and my voice to help to create change. There is a negative outlook on addiction and I have to show the community that humans can change. The opiate epidemic is getting worse. Too many people are dying. I will not stop showing the world that recovery is possible and I will not stop trying to help humans like me. Helping myself and growing in life is something I did and still do in order to be an example to others. I love helping the women at McShin, especially the moms. Another cool thing I get to do is go into jails and be a hope dealer to women that are incarcerated, that is freaking awesome!!

After taking eight years to fix my credit, we were finally able to buy our first home. It was difficult trying to find a house we could afford that also had the things we wanted. After touring a few, we finally found our perfect little home. All I really wanted was a porch to put rocking chairs on and everyone to have their own room. *Ding, Ding! We had a winner.* I was in love as soon as we pulled into the driveway. When we walked in, I immediately felt at home and knew this would be ours. Days later, it was. I couldn't believe that we were homeowners. Crying and feeling warm inside happened immediately. *Is this our life? Seriously, Did we just BUY a house?*

Entering into McShin all those years ago, I told myself that I would never be able to fix my credit, I was a bit of a bummer in early recovery. Well, hard work, financial management, and the drive to want more for my family made it all happen. Our kids and our dog, Jax loved it. We settled in and became part of the neighborhood. We are still in this home today and I don't ever want to leave. It is precious, simple, and holds so much love.

My career was getting bigger. *Who knew I could make a career out of my experiences being addicted to heroin and other drugs?* Things started to change and I started to really grow as one of the leaders at McShin, as a woman leader. Being a leader is great, but I wanted to learn more. I applied for Stanford's Executive Nonprofit Leadership Program. Yikes, here came all of my negative self-talk. *You are never getting in. You are not that smart. You suck, get real. Guess who got in? Shut up negative Nancy!* The program was only for one week, but it was everything to me. Honesty Liller was in college. I learned a lot; the campus was gorgeous; and I got to meet so many cool leaders from around the world. *You just need to try things to see what you can accomplish. Always remind yourself that you are smart, you can do hard things, and you are a badass! That's what I do constantly to this day.*

After that, John and I got invited to be on *Face The Nation. Wowzers!* The whole experience was awesome, except the makeup. I didn't realize how much damn makeup you needed to be on TV.

I felt like it took me days to get it off when we were done. *You can find a little bit of eyeliner on this gorgeous face on a regular day and maybe some mascara if I am feeling fancy. God bless all you TV and movie stars!* When John Dickerson told me that they had four million viewers right before the camera was rolling, my throat gulped and I said to myself, "Let's go!" It was only about four minutes of content but we expressed what needed to be said. Humans are dying; families are getting torn apart; WE NEED YOUR HELP.

Being a face and voice for change is something that I never thought I would do. Now, I love it and will keep doing it until I no longer have a voice. When you get close to people and see them try recovery but then they overdose and die, it is heartbreaking.

John and I started our own company to become an even louder voice. It is called CARE Talks and we have eight speakers at each event educating the audience on addiction solutions. *Running a company is challenging in itself but I go with the flow and keep learning. I am a female entrepreneur. Let me say that again, "I am a female entrepreneur."* **There is a God; there is a spirit filled energy; and there is hope.** Receiving awards and being recognized for what I do naturally is pretty cool. I never thought that would happen in any area of my life, especially as a child or during my addiction. But being recognized feels pretty damn good. It is not because I am someone that is super important, but it is because I am me. In order to survive in this world, I have to be my authentic self.

One winter, I was trying everything to live the life I wanted and thought I deserved but there was nothing I could do to get out of this funk I was in. I was talking, praying, running, exercising, talking, talking, talking, and nothing worked. After reading some things about winter depression, I basically diagnosed myself. It was a weird time for me because I was trying to help people and I couldn't help myself. It wasn't fun. Then I started to take Vitamin D and eat healthier. *I be damned, that worked. Winter depression is real and if you think you get it, talk to someone immediately. It is just so dark and cold. I am a bright and warm type of chick.* Now to prepare for winter, I have everyday practices I do in my life to assure if that happens again, I have a plan. This was a few years ago and I have not experienced it since. *Don't give up on yourself and reach out for help.*

Adam came to me one day and said he wanted to start his own business. I knew in his heart he wanted to but this was the real, real conversation. There was so much running through my head. *How will he help with bills? Will he be gone all the time?* I like to know our budget and I am a planner for the most part. So, this sketched me out but I said go for it and he did. We haven't looked back yet. He has had some growing pains and I have been along for the ride. But, seeing your partner's dreams come true is priceless and I am so very proud of him.

Also, going through my head was...*Am I following my dreams?* I had the kids, the house, the career, and the friends. *But, was there more?* Day in and day out living life is what we do. I had been working at McShin basically my whole recovery and this has been the longest job I have ever held. *Helping humans, especially moms is my purpose on this earth and it feels great doing it.* McShin is my second home and sometimes work life has conflicts. John and I went through some growing pains in our relationship. *Being with someone most of your daily life for over ten years comes with personality clashes.* Our jobs are stressful and demanding most of the time.

Imagine years of this. The good news is that he and I sought professional help. Our relationship is so positive now and we are continuing to grow individually, as well as the leaders of the organization. *Life can be rocky but there is always a way through the rocks. Or you just pick them up and throw them at one another, just kidding! Seeking help in order to better yourself is something that everyone should try if they need it. It is a life changer. There are so many things that I do now to help my mind be at peace that are healthy for me.*

For example, following inspiring women on Instagram is a big one, I love seeing so many women changing the world. One of my faves is "Whataldenate". She is one of my dear friends and watching her follow her dreams helps me follow mine. *Thanks, Aldo!* Women rule and it took me a while to realize how awesome we truly are. Some things I thought were: women cook, clean, take care of the kids, listen, and get judged. Some things I know are: women can cook, clean, take care of their kids, listen, and be judged, but who gives a shit? We can be entrepreneurs, healers, and a zillion other things. Society puts so much pressure on women and I refuse to be a part of that culture anymore. Adam helps me with this constantly by being my partner, not just what society tells us a husband should be. *That shit is lame....YEARS of my life I tried to live up to what society thought. Not today sister, not today.*

"A dog is a man's best friend" and "Diamonds are a girl's best friend" are common cliches but diamonds aren't my jam and my dog is my best friend. I declared that I wanted a Yorkie for years! When the day came that I found her, I knew that my thoughts and words had manifested her. We went to get her and when I saw her in person, I fell in love. There in front of me was Shelby Monroe Liller. Some think dogs are just dogs, but I am telling you she has gotten me through so many tough times and has been my angel for a few years now. *However, getting and training a puppy comes with very high stress and little sleep. Since I didn't want any more human kids, why not get a doggie one?* Well, this really took a toll on my spirit for real. I loved her, but the potty training sucked so much. Those few months were torture and I had to push through.

Apologizing was my motto at the time and I had to pray hard. *What can I say? I am not a perfect human and I don't like shit on my carpet.* There, I said it. She is now alone since Jax passed and we are talking about getting her a sibling. *Hmmm....maybe I should keep praying on this one?*

God knows I love her, but a new puppy? Well, I am in a completely different mindset than I was a few years ago when she joined our family. *We shall see.*

Writing this book has been on my heart for some time. Watching amazing women follow their dreams and seeing many female authors changing the world, I was inspired to do so. I wanted to reach even more women and help even more moms. One day, I had a woman do an energy cleanse on me and she told me that I would write the book. My heart fluttered, but my mind said, "When will you have time to do this?" *Blah, Blah, shut it!* This got me thinking and I wanted to learn more. So I started this program my friend, Sara Daves, teaches called "Manifest Like A Goddess". *Oh yeah, here we go!* The things I learned about myself and how to release my spirit changed my perspective on life. There was a deeper connection between my brain and my heart. *Then I knew, I would write this damn book...one day.*

There is something else that I want to accomplish while I am on this planet. And that is, to show my daughter that she is worth the world and whatever she wants out of it. Additionally, to teach my son to treat women equally and we don't have time for any sexist bullshit.

The day Destiny graduated from high school was epic. I don't remember my graduation day because I was high and to be a part of her life without being high is freaking incredible! This was during COVID-19 and it was so intimate how the school set it up, I loved it! No traffic, there weren't hundreds of people, just us with our amazing daughter.

We teach our kids to follow their hearts and learn about themselves along the way. Being a parent is hard, but also it is the best thing I can do on this earth. Children are the future of our world. Show them that life is hard; you don't always win; if you work hard you may succeed; and if someone knocks you down you get the "F" back up. You can cry and eat lots of ice cream, that's cool too. I challenge you to find your people. Find those who will love you for you. Those who will laugh with you, cry with you, and tell you when you are being off the chain.

Life is way too short to not live it. So, get up and go live.

CHAPTER 13

A HAPPY LIFE IS A HEALING LIFE

The more life kept going, I started to take a look around and wasn't comfortable in my own presence. I wanted to remain positive constantly; I wanted to listen to all the advice I gave everyone else; but something wasn't working. It is hard having a role at your job and a role in the community that you are supposed to live up to. *Well, I am here to tell you that I had a legit midlife crisis or whatever the hell you want to call it.*

I was grieving over the deaths from overdose in our community. Some were friends and some I knew from McShin. Regardless, it really started to take a toll on me. I was overtaken with deep sadness and found myself crying a lot. *Was I helping? Am I going to stay at McShin forever and keep feeling this heartache?* There were so many questions that I was trying to answer, but just couldn't. Every day, I would talk to God and ask for some form of clarity. I would release my pain to Spirit and ask to be healed. But the skies didn't open up, and there was no rainbow.

My day to day home life was making me want more out

of life or just something different. Work, dinner, sleep, and repeat was messing with my brain. My body image issues kicked into high gear again along with all of my fears. *When I don't like myself is when I take it out on others...usually those closest to me.* My emotions were all over the place. There was no controlling them. In recovery, I am taught to reach out to my support network, which I did. The thoughts in my head were running all around like they just ate a pound of sugar.

We all go through seasons in our life. *This season was dark for me, but my hair was pink, so that added some flare.* I tried different forms of exercise and diets, like shakes and other things that you see on social media. Throughout my recovery, I fell for many different things to change the way my body looked. Some worked for a couple of months and some not at all. Expecting my body to look like someone else's is unrealistic. *More on that in the last chapter.* With my addictive brain, I wanted to quickly fix my emotions. What I did was work, work, add stuff to my calendar, and add more stuff. I was telling myself, "FILL THAT VOID, Honesty." *Fill it with shit that you don't even need to do. If you are feeling stuck in your life right now, stop and write down some things you are grateful for. I don't have all the answers for everyone's situation but I can share with you mine.*

The void needed to be filled and I didn't want to fill it with drugs. *Did I want attention? What the hell was going on? I truly appreciated my life, but there was something off.* Not sure what was going on in my mind but I felt like I was possessed like Billy from *Stranger Things*. My body was there but my heart and mind weren't. There was so much pain bottled up inside of me and I didn't know what to do and really didn't know why. I tried all the healthy routes, but nothing was working. *Was I unhappy? Yes, yes, I was.* This realization came to a crashing halt when I told my husband. There were things that we needed to change, things I needed to change. Saying these words out loud broke my heart as well as his. But, they needed to be said. I needed to live and be real with him. Trying to unpack my feelings and figure out what I was actually feeling was very hard for me. *Let them sit, let them resonate, let them shine.* Being in recovery and working through my past has helped but this season of my life, nothing was helping. It was up to me, my God, and those that love me to figure it out.

My girls…I have a few that are my ride or die and have been with me for years. Rachel and McKenzie have been in my life since I found recovery. Stacy has been on the scene for over five years now. YOU NEED TO FIND your people. These women have not only listened to me throughout all my seasons of life, they have guided me in the path of change and acceptance. I needed them more than ever during this season and they did not disappoint. Rachel was my sponsor for twelve years. Her best advice at this time was to change some major things in my life that were doable and healthy. So, I got a new sponsor that week. Rachel did what she could for me and is still one of the closest humans to my heart, but I needed a different perspective from another woman that was a stranger to me. *Start from scratch!* McKenzie helped me see that I deserved all the love in the world and that includes loving myself. Stacy's soul is kind and sweet. And her laugh…I love her laugh, I needed to laugh. Last but not least, Kelli is one of those friends that I will have for the rest of my life. No matter how much time passes, we love each other as friends so deeply that I know that love will be there forever. She frustrates me, makes me laugh, helps my kids, and helps me even though there is always some kind of drama. Kelli, you are one of a kind. *Thank you ladies, thank you! This is the stuff I tell women on the daily, why in the hell did I not listen to my own voice?* As humans we can get stuck. This was hard for me to fathom because I was so far along in my recovery life, but I had to look in the mirror and tell myself, "let's go deeper."

My marriage was rocky; I was rocky; and I don't mean Balboa. Adam and I started marriage therapy immediately. *At first I was like, ew...therapy. I just thought of my favorite show in the world typing that. Ew...David, to all my Schitt's Creek fans out there, love ya!* Back to therapy. I hadn't been since after my overdose when I was young. This time would be different. I was open-minded and I wanted to make some changes. We needed someone else to help us dig deep into what we were both feeling.

Everyone would tell me that marriage was work and I thought I knew what that meant. I did not, until now. *Having a woman therapist meant that she would be on my side, right?* After our first session, I was wrong. I thought she was on both of our sides. But in reality, she was on neither of our sides. She helped us see each other's pain, childhood trauma, and how to communicate our feelings to one another. *Like REALLY communicate our feelings.* I've honestly changed my view on therapy. *I say go...if you feel you need to. It was literally life-changing.*

For us, it changed our perspective on our life together, and thank God it did. It was hard to learn how to truly communicate and respect your partner's feelings, especially when I thought I had been doing that the whole damn time. *Well, HELLO, no you weren't, sister.* We learned so much about each other that we didn't know. *Like I thought I knew, but I really didn't know.* This is the only life that I get to have and I am going to keep developing my soul. Adam deserves the same. He is not only my husband, but he is my best friend. Therapy transformed our awesome life into a much happier place. I am beyond excited to sit in our rocking chairs on our porch for the rest of our lives here on Earth.

Since meeting in rehab, which feels like 100 years ago now, our love story has been interesting to say the least. *But it is our story, and that is special to me.* Along with therapy, we made a pact to spend more time together, go on dates, and spend at least a weekend away every few months. Recently, we just decided on a new thing. We are both early birds and while we enjoy our coffee together, we tend to talk about "big life shit (BLS)". *That is what I like to call it.* BLS should not be talked about at 6 am. So, our solution is if either of us starts BLS, then we get to say "big life shit" out loud. Then we both stop, maybe kiss, and go on with our morning routines.

One of our first trips away was to a cabin on top of a mountain. *BEAUTIFUL!* But before we got there, we decided to hike Old Rag Mountain in Madison County, VA. I love nature. *Well most of it, bugs aren't my jam.* Hiking and running outside are two of my favorite things to do. For him to hike with me was a change and I loved it! When I think of hiking, I think of walking up a big hill with leaves all around and beautiful scenery. This mountain had all of that, but it also had huge boulders you had to climb too. Clearly, we did not know what we were getting into. At some point climbing up, we looked at each other and said, "Well, we can't quit now." Adam literally had to catch me while I jumped to him from a boulder. I felt like a spider monkey and prayed he would catch me. Obviously, he did. When we got to the top of that mountain, we took in one of the most amazing views I have ever seen in my life. As we hugged, I realized that this was more than a hike, this was a healing process for us. We went back down the mountain another way because we just weren't ready to die that day. *Grateful hearts, and smart brains too.*

Finally, our marriage was in a beautiful place and I started to incorporate all the things I love back into my life. This time they weren't things I "had" to do, these were things I wanted to do. One was running a half marathon. Running 10K's was all I thought I could do. When people said to me, "Why don't you run a marathon or a half marathon?" The negative Nancy in my brain would shout, "YOU CANNOT DO THAT, YOU SUCK." Well, I said, "'F' her!" I started running more and more and more. Completing my first half marathon was one of the biggest highlights of my life. Some can run with ease, but I worked hard for this day. Running is part of my own self-care and mental health. It has helped me make many better decisions for my life. There is nothing like going through some drama or life issues and just running it out. My favorite run is on a beach watching the dolphins in the ocean and the beautiful sun hitting the water like diamonds. The beach is one of my serene, talk to God places. I started the McShin Run Club, and we run once a week together. There are just a few of us but my dream is to build a whole running recovery community. Running from drug dealers was what I used to do, now I run for me. *It works, try it, or walk fast, something.* Exercise releases emotions and literally can help you solve your life problems. *Well, maybe not solve everything, but it sure helps.* Not only did I complete that half marathon with a time that was freakin' incredible, but Adam and Wyatt waited in the cold for me at the finish line. Seeing them coming at me for a hug after I crossed that line made me want to cry. But it was so cold, I had to keep on moving. They are the best and I love being able to show my son that with hard work, anything is possible. *So, if all else fails, Run Forrest Run.*

To be your happiest self; forgive, love, and forgive some more. Love is love and all you can do is embrace it.

CHAPTER 14

EW COVID

When COVID hit, the addiction crisis got worse. We kept our doors open at McShin from the beginning of the shutdowns, so it was a lot on myself and our staff. But, we have an amazing team, and it brought us all closer. For someone to be isolated and have an addiction usually doesn't end well. We thrive on hugs and connection. Humans with addiction needed us more than ever. Meanwhile, I was trying to figure out how to live in this new world. Wyatt was in fifth grade and Destiny was a senior in high school when the school system shut down. Adam and I were like *WTF*. The whole United States was like that too, I assume. For the first few weeks, we pushed through. I am fortunate that I can do most of my job duties from home. Wyatt was able to be beside me at our dining table doing his school work. It was hard being at home all day, every day. My husband had to leave every day because he is a landscaper. *But nope, not me.* My focus was on trying to find funds for McShin to survive in case the shit hit the fan. So, I did. Zoom meetings became my friend. I would zoom into one of our female houses every other day and tried my best to help the women. After weeks of zoom meetings and zooming everything, I was zoomed out. But, I had to do it, I had to help the best way I could. This took a toll on my own personal recovery. It was the first time in years that I had really thought about using heroin, or even smoking weed. Times were tough and the world as I knew it was ending. *Ok, I am being dramatic, but times were tough.* The cool part about recovery from addiction...is that I know how to talk about it when I want to use. My girls and I started a weekly zoom to check in with life.

Ladies, you helped save me! Soon, the thoughts of using passed. Amazing music really helped me as well. I consider music a pathway of my personal recovery journey. Artists like Demi Lovato, The Avett Brothers, and Bob Marley helped get me through this too. There is nothing like riding down the road, blaring your tunes, and singing as loud as you can. I even dance sometimes too, of course very carefully while driving.

As I am writing about COVID, I actually have COVID. I am sitting on my porch outside in my rocking chair as I type this on my last day of quarantine. COVID is a bitch but I am through the worst of it, thank you God. Watching the news really isn't my jam, so my husband and colleagues will usually fill me in on the latest things. There are so many opinions and views on this topic. Instead of getting overwhelmed, I logged off of all platforms and chose to watch *Schitt's Creek* so I could laugh my ass off. *I am actually a little obsessed and have watched it six times since COVID hit in 2020.*

Having COVID has changed my perspective. During the fifteen days that I have been sick, there was one day that was super scary and my anxiety was through the roof. I made a promise to myself to truly go back to living one day at a time. I was thinking about writing this book before COVID hit the world, but I REALLY started talking about it in March of

2020. I would talk and dream, then talk and dream some more. Then one day, I kept talking about it with Adam. He looked at me and said, "Write the damn book." *Thanks honey, love you!* That got me to really manifest writing this book and truly believing that I will help at least one, maybe ten, maybe 1,000 humans on this earth. Here I am almost completing this dream. *Manifestation and prayer work, I am living proof.*

There is a list of several things I tried to do to "fix" myself throughout my whole life: lie, steal, drugs, alcohol, pretending to be someone else, exercise, diets, doing things I didn't want to do, and honestly being nice to people that didn't deserve it. While all those things have helped to guide me into being the woman I am today, I believe loving yourself enough to be yourself is the most important thing I have learned. And the best part, I am excited to continue to learn even more about myself.

Turning forty last year was amazing. Our culture teaches us that when you are a forty-year-old woman, you are old, need botox, or need to get ready for the next half of your life. *I threw all those stereotypes out the damn window!* Embracing my age is something I am very grateful for...I should be dead. The value of being on Earth and trying to make a difference is priceless not only in my career, but in my home, in writing this book, and in speaking up for change. Forty looks and feels beautiful on me. Who would've thought I would ever love myself as I do. *If I can, so can you!* After I hit the big 4-0, I made a few changes. First, the smartwatch that I wore to track my running, calories, steps, even my damn breathing was removed from my wrist and I haven't had it on for months. For me, that watch brought anxiety, self-doubt, shame, and feelings that I don't even care to have in my world. *You Gotta Go Yo!* Also, it was such a sense of freedom to not be at someone's beck and call. Every. Single. Text. Would vibrate my arm. *Nope, not today!* With this newfound freedom *(insert Mel Gibson as William Wallace, every time I hear that word "freedom"...EVERY TIME),* I learned how to truly love my body. It is literally the only one I am going to get, so why the hell not? After years of trying to get a shape or a look, now I believe I wasn't made to have it which has made this year invigorating and inspiring. Second, my daily routine is something I cherish. Waking up, coffee, journaling, walking Shelby Monroe, and then some form of exercise that I actually enjoy. Some mornings, I just sit on the couch with Adam and watch the news. Those days I usually stretch a lot, walk Shelby longer or do yoga with my white sage incense smoking up the room. I have always wanted a she-sanctuary outside to be used as a little gym/writing room. We just can't afford that right now, so I have accepted that and transformed Wyatt's playroom into my gym. *He is now twelve and doesn't need a baby playroom.* It works perfectly for my meditation and exercise time. It was super inexpensive to fix up and I love it.

"Work with what I have" is my motto. I don't have many things and I like it that way. My goal in life is to enjoy more experiences with those that I love, not collect things that I would just end up giving away. I like the simple life and I am happy that Adam does too. After learning how to meditate and sit in silence, I found that there was so much more out of life that I wanted.

No matter what I have gone through in this interesting life, forgiving myself on a daily basis is still necessary. This past year has taught me a lot of things, but the biggest thing is forgiveness. Whether it is from the pain in my past or having thoughts about people that are straight-up assholes, I know I need to continually give myself grace and try to do the right thing by forgiving. This isn't always easy, but it is something I work hard on and still need to.

Additionally, writing in my journals, following amazing humans on social media, and having the best friends and family in the universe helps me each day. *Go look in the mirror and say, "I forgive and love you." I am telling you it works. It is not a magic mirror, you do need to work on your soul, but it is the start to an amazing life.*

My marriage is blossoming every day. The relationship that Adam and I have is one of hope and resilience. He is my best friend and I thank God for him. While I have been sick with COVID, he literally is living out the meaning of "in sickness and in health" by taking care of me every day. Our life isn't perfect but it is pretty damn close. This takes a lot of work, forgiveness, laughs, hope, grace, and above all, love. Our kids have seen our love, fears, and sense of hope.

Destiny is now in college and working at a daycare. *SHE IS IN COLLEGE. I never went to college, well that one week in Stanford, let's not forget that...hello...Stanford.* I am very proud of the woman she is becoming and the relationship that we have. When she was born in withdrawal from heroin, I never even dreamed I would be alive to see her in college or to feel the love that she has for me. I am blessed beyond measure because of my recovery and my willingness to change. *I love you, Des.*

Wyatt is a special blessing as well. I didn't want another child because of the whole Hepatitis C thing but I am so glad God had other plans. Watching my boy play baseball on his travel team is something that never gets old. His love for me and his big laugh melts my heart. Our daily morning walks with Shelby...And him talking, talking, and talking...I don't ever want those times to stop. He will always be mommy's lil' sweetie! *I love you, Y!*

Everyone that knows me, knows *Elf* is my favorite movie of all time. There is something magical about Christmas that makes me feel like a kid. *Santa is real and you can't tell me differently.* I think I love it so much because even though I felt like my childhood was somewhat depressing, my parents always made Christmas special. The love that comes with the spirit of Christmas is something I wish the world could have all year round. Although I can't smell because of COVID right now, my mind is smelling a fresh Christmas tree. Having a real tree is part of the magic of holidays for me, along with the memories it brings. There were so many years where I was not present either physically or emotionally during the holidays. *SO MANY YEARS.* Now, I cherish all the time I get to spend with my family and friends. Having actual good memories is what I love the most. When I was using, the holidays were sad for me and I did so many horrible things. Feeling like a kid again makes my heart warm. Christmas is magic and I will always value my love for it. Also, I love to show those new to recovery that they can be loved and feel the love during the holidays. *My wish for you is to find joy, find love, and find out what life means to you.*

The relationships I have with all of my parents, my two sisters, and my three brothers have healed. I thank God all the time that I am not putting them through any more pain. Me and my sisters are wives and moms. We get to help each other and live this life together, grow together as women. Families can heal and family is forever.

As an adult in recovery, I was interviewed by a CNN reporter recently. She asked me if my childhood trauma was the reason I started using drugs. All my years using and even in my recovery, I never blamed that decision on my parents. I chose to use drugs. But as I was answering the reporter, I started to ask myself the same question. The freedom I had as a child was a contributing factor and being able to cover up my drug use was a special skill. Yet, I still don't blame anyone for my choices. I just wanted to be someone else. *Sure, I could sit here... have this pain, carry this pain, and live this pain.* But I choose to learn, love, and live the best damn life I can while I am here on Earth.

Life can be hard. Life can be challenging. Life can be loud. Life can be scary. Life can be amazing. Life can be love. We have this one life, go live it.

ACKNOWLEDGEMENTS

My first born Destiny, thank you for teaching me how to be a mother. I am forever grateful for your forgiveness. You make my life full and you are going to do amazing things in this world. I am beyond proud of the woman you are becoming and I thank God for your every day. Thank you for making me a mother.

My favorite son, Wyatt, you came into this world from true love. Your heart and laughter make me smile. You teach me patience, acceptance, and how to forgive myself on the regular. The love I have for you will be eternal and you will always be Mommy's Lil' Sweetie!

To my sisters, Zin and Harmony, we will forever be bonded. Thank you for all the laughs and great memories we can share forever. I am proud to be your sister and to share this life with you. Shoes!

To all of my parents, I would like to thank you for loving me. I wouldn't be alive without your faith and your support of my recovery. I appreciate all of you and the way you touch my life. You are the most amazing grandparents too and I am so grateful that you show my kids what true love is. Thank You!

All my bros, Dougie, Mikey, and Hutt, I am so glad God brought you into my life. All three of you make our family fun and complete.

John and Carol, thank you for opening a safe place for those like me to start their recovery journeys. I will forever be grateful to you and McShin's mission. I love you both dearly and thank you for being authentic leaders that have helped me through this thing called life.

Rachel, McKenzie, Kelli, Stacy, and Alden ...A girl couldn't ask for better friends. You all have helped me in so many ways for so many years. Your hearts are huge and I am so grateful to live this life with you. Thank you for teaching me how to love myself, feel my feelings, and how to be a mommy. Love you ladies!

Women leaders and writers...To all the amazing women and writers that I have been following for years. Thank you for showing me that I have a voice and I can use it to do good in this world. You Rock!

To all the recovery warriors and advocates out there. I understand you. I hear you.....keep roaring!

KWE Publishing, Maria and Kim, thank you for showing up in my life when I needed to kickstart this writing process. Maria you have been amazing to work with and have helped this woman become an author. THANK YOU!!!

Adam...Thank you for loving me. You are my biggest fan and I will forever love you for that. Being your wife helps me love myself and accept myself for who I am. Your heart is huge and I would not be writing this book without your support. I will climb any mountain with you any day! I will be your boo forever.

RESOURCES

Resources and some amazing humans that have helped me

The McShin Foundation www.mcshin.org 804-249-1845
    Recovery Community Organization in Richmond, VA that is accredited by CAPRSS. McShin has thirteen recovery homes that help humans with addiction as well as recovery jail programs, family programs, and faith based programs..

Get In The Herd **Podcast Spotify, iHeart Radio, McShin's Facebook page**

CARE Talks, LLC
    www.caretalks.net

Impower Experience, McKenzie Payne
    https://www.theimpowerexperience.com

Awesome Instagram Ladies:
    whataldenate jeneppfit annabdavid

Ryan Hampton
Ryanhampton.org

The Voices Project Instagram: voicesriseup

Sara Daves
saradaves.com

Percilla Zeno
www.percillazeno.com

Narcotics Anonymous
www.na.org

Printed in the USA
CPSIA information can be obtained
at www.ICGtesting.com
BVHW020915290823
668951BV00002B/7